LESSONS IN MUSIC FORM

A MANUAL OF

ANALYSIS

OF ALL THE STRUCTURAL FACTORS AND DESIGNS
EMPLOYED IN MUSICAL COMPOSITION

BY

PERCY GOETSCHIUS, MUS. DOC.
(Royal Württemberg Professor)

AUTHOR OF

THE MATERIAL USED IN MUSICAL COMPOSITION, THE THEORY AND PRACTICE OF TONE-RELATIONS
THE HOMOPHONIC FORMS OF MUSICAL COMPOSITION, MODELS OF THE PRINCIPAL MUSIC
FORMS, EXERCISES IN MELODY WRITING, APPLIED COUNTERPOINT, ETC.

GREENWOOD PRESS, PUBLISHERS
WESTPORT, CONNECTICUT

122984

Originally published in 1904
by Oliver Ditson Company, Philadelphia

First Greenwood Reprinting 1970

Library of Congress Catalogue Card Number 79-109735

SBN 8371-4225-3

Printed in the United States of America

FOREWORD.

THE present manual treats of the structural designs of musical composition, not of the styles or species of music. Read our AFTERWORD.

It undertakes the thorough explanation of each design or form, from the smallest to the largest ; and such comparison as serves to demonstrate the principle of natural evolution, in the operation of which the entire system originates.

This explanation — be it well understood — is conducted solely with a view to the *Analysis* of musical works, and is not calculated to prepare the student for the application of form in practical composition. For the exhaustive exposition of the technical apparatus, the student must be referred to my " Homophonic Forms."

The present aim is to enable the student to recognize and trace the mental process of the composer in executing his task ; to define each factor of the structural design, and its relation to every other factor and to the whole ; to determine thus the synthetic meaning of the work, and thereby to increase not only his own appreciation, interest, and enjoyment of the very real beauties of good music, but also his power to *interpret*, intelligently and adequately, the works that engage his attention.

*　*　*

The choice of classic literature to which most frequent reference is made, and which the student is therefore expected to procure before beginning his lessons, includes : —

The Songs Without Words of Mendelssohn ; the *Jugend*

Album, Op. 68, of Schumann ; the pianoforte sonatas of Mozart (Peters edition) ; the pianoforte sonatas of Beethoven.

Besides these, incidental reference is made to the symphonies of Beethoven, the sonatas of Schubert, the mazurkas of Chopin, and other pianoforte compositions of Mendelssohn, Beethoven, Chopin, and Brahms.

PERCY GOETSCHIUS.

BOSTON, MASS., *Sept.,* 1904.

TABLE OF CONTENTS.

CHAPTER I. — INTRODUCTION.

PAGE

THE NECESSITY OF FORM IN MUSIC 1
THE EVIDENCES OF FORM IN MUSIC 3
UNITY AND VARIETY 5

CHAPTER II. — FUNDAMENTAL DETAILS.

TIME 11
TEMPO 11
BEATS 11
MEASURES 12
RHYTHM 13
MELODY 14

CHAPTER III. — FIGURE AND MOTIVE.

THE MELODIC FIGURE 19
DEFINING THE FIGURES 20
THE MELODIC MOTIVE, OR PHRASE-MEMBER 22
PRELIMINARY TONES 25

CHAPTER IV. — THE PHRASE.

THE PHRASE 30
LENGTH OF THE REGULAR PHRASE 31
EXCEPTIONS 33
CONTENTS OF THE PHRASE 35

CHAPTER V. — CADENCES.

CADENCES IN GENERAL 37
MODIFICATION, OR DISGUISING OF THE CADENCE 38
THE ELISION 46
SPECIES OF CADENCE 50
PERFECT CADENCE 51
SEMICADENCE 55
LOCATING THE CADENCES 58

▼

CHAPTER VI. — IRREGULAR PHRASES.

Page

CAUSES OF IRREGULARITY 60
THE SMALL AND LARGE PHRASES 60
THE PRINCIPLE OF EXTENSION 62
INHERENT IRREGULARITY 67

CHAPTER VII. — THE PERIOD-FORM.

PHRASE-ADDITION 69
THE PERIOD 69

CHAPTER VIII. — ENLARGEMENT OF THE PERIOD-FORM.

ENLARGEMENT BY REPETITION 75
THE PHRASE-GROUP 77
THE DOUBLE-PERIOD 80

CHAPTER IX. — THE TWO-PART SONG-FORM.

THE SONG-FORM, OR PART-FORM 83
THE PARTS 84
THE FIRST PART 85
THE SECOND PART 85

CHAPTER X. — THE THREE-PART SONG-FORM.

DISTINCTION BETWEEN BIPARTITE AND TRIPARTITE FORMS 89
PART I 90
PART II 90
PART III 91

CHAPTER XI. — ENLARGEMENT OF THE THREE-PART SONG-FORM.

REPETITION OF THE PARTS 96
EXACT REPETITIONS 96
MODIFIED REPETITIONS 97
THE FIVE-PART FORM 98
GROUP OF PARTS 99

CHAPTER XII. — THE SONG-FORM WITH TRIO.

THE PRINCIPAL SONG 101
THE TRIO, OR SUBORDINATE SONG 101
THE "DA CAPO" 101

CHAPTER XIII. — THE FIRST RONDO-FORM.

EVOLUTION 105
THE RONDO-FORMS 106
THE FIRST RONDO-FORM 108

CHAPTER XIV. — The Second Rondo-form.

PAGE

DETAILS 115

CHAPTER XV. — The Third Rondo-form.

THE EXPOSITION 117
THE MIDDLE DIVISION 118
THE RECAPITULATION 118

CHAPTER XVI. — The Sonatine-form.

CLASSIFICATION OF THE LARGER FORMS 121
THE SONATINE-FORM 122

CHAPTER XVII. — The Sonata-allegro Form.

ORIGIN OF THE NAME 124
THE SONATA-ALLEGRO FORM 124
THE EXPOSITION 125
THE DEVELOPMENT, OR MIDDLE DIVISION 125
THE RECAPITULATION 126
DISSOLUTION 127
RELATION TO THE THREE-PART SONG-FORM 132

CHAPTER XVIII. — Irregular Forms.

CAUSES 136
AUGMENTATION OF THE REGULAR FORM 137
ABBREVIATION OF THE REGULAR FORM 138
DISLOCATION OF THEMATIC MEMBERS 139
MIXTURE OF CHARACTERISTIC TRAITS 139

CHAPTER XIX. — Application of the Forms.

APPLICATION OF THE SEVERAL DESIGNS IN PRACTICAL COMPOSITION . . 142
AFTERWORD 146

LESSONS IN MUSIC FORM.

CHAPTER I. INTRODUCTION.

The Necessity of Form in Music. — So much uncertainty and diversity of opinion exists among music lovers of every grade concerning the presence of Form in musical composition, and the necessity of its presence there, that a few general principles are submitted at the outset of our studies, as a guide to individual reflection and judgment on the subject.

Certain apparently defensible prejudices that prevail in the minds of even advanced musical critics against the idea of Form in music, originate in a very manifest mistake on the part of the "formalists" themselves, who (I refer to unimpassioned theorists and advocates of rigid old scholastic rules) place too narrow a construction upon Form, and define it with such rigor as to leave no margin whatever for the exercise of free fancy and emotional sway. Both the dreamer, with his indifference to (or downright scorn of) Form; and the pedant, with his narrow conception of it; as well as the ordinary music lover, with his endeavor to discover some less debatable view to adopt for his own everyday use, — need to be reminded *that Form in music means simply Order in music.*

Thus interpreted, the necessity of form, that is, Order, in the execution of a musical design appears as obvious as are the laws of architecture to the builder, or the laws of creation to the astronomer or naturalist; for the absence of order, that is, Disorder, constitutes a condition which is regarded with abhorrence and dread by every rational mind.

3

A musical composition, then, in which Order prevails; in which all the factors are chosen and treated in close keeping with their logical bearing upon each other and upon the whole; in which, in a word, there is no disorder of thought or technique, — is music with Form (*i.e.* good Form). A sensible arrangement of the various members of the composition (its figures, phrases, motives, and the like) will exhibit both agreement and contrast, both confirmation and opposition ; for we measure things by comparison with both like and unlike. Our nature demands the evi dence of *uniformity*, as that emphasizes the impressions, making them easier to grasp and enjoy; but our nature also craves a certain degree of *variety*, to counteract the monotony which must result from too persistent uniformity. When the elements of Unity and Variety are sensibly matched, evenly balanced, the form is good. On the other hand, a composition is formless, or faulty in form, when the component parts are jumbled together without regard to proportion and relation.

Which of these two conditions is the more desirable, or necessary, would seem to be wholly self-evident.

The error made by pedantic teachers is to demand *too much* Form ; to insist that a piece of music shall be a model of arithmetical adjustment. This is probably a graver error than apparent formlessness. Design and logic and unity there must surely be ; but any *obtrusive* evidence of mathematical calculation must degrade music to the level of a mere handicraft.

* * *

Another and higher significance involved in the idea of Form, that goes to prove how indispensable it may be in truly good music, rests upon the opposition of Form to the material.

There are two essentially different classes of music lovers : — the one class takes delight in the mere sound and jingle of the music; not looking for any higher purpose than this, they content themselves with the purely sensuous enjoyment that the sound material affords. To such listeners, a comparatively meaningless succession of tones and chords is sufficiently enjoyable, so long as each separate particle, each beat or measure, is euphonious in itself. The other class, more discriminating in its tastes, looks beneath this iridescent surface and strives to fathom the under-lying *purpose* of it all ; not content with the testimony of the ear alone, such hearers enlist the higher, nobler powers of Reason, and no amount of pleasant sounds could compensate them for the absence of well-ordered parts and their logical justification.

This second class is made up of those listeners who recognize in music an embodiment of artistic aims, an object of serious and refined enjoyment *that appeals to the emotions through the intelligence,* — not a plaything for the senses alone ; and who believe that all music that would in this sense be truly artistic, must exhibit " Form " as the end, and " Material " only as a means to this end.

* * *

Still another, and possibly the strongest argument of all for the necessity of form in music, is derived from reflection upon the peculiarly vague and intangible nature of its art-material — tone, sound. The words of a language (also sounds, it is true) have established meanings, so familiar and definite that they recall and re-awaken impressions of thought and action with a vividness but little short of the actual experience. Tones, on the contrary, are not and cannot be associated with any *definite* ideas or impressions ; they are as impalpable as they are transient, and, taken separately, leave no lasting trace.

Therefore, whatever stability and palpability a musical composition is to acquire, *must be derived from its form, or design,* and not from its totally unsubstantial material. It must fall back upon the network traced by the disposition of its points and lines upon the musical canvas ; for this it is that constitutes its real and palpable contents.

The Evidences of Form in Music. — The presence of form in music is manifested, first of all, by the disposition of tones and chords in symmetrical measures, and by the numerous methods of tone arrangement which create and define the element of Rhythm, — the distinction of short and long time-values, and of accented and unaccented (that is, heavy and light) pulses.

This is not what is commonly supposed to constitute form in music, but it is the fundamental condition out of which an orderly system of form may be developed. As well might the carpenter or architect venture to dispense with scale, compass and square in their constructive labors, as that the composer should neglect beat, measure and rhythm, in his effort to realize a well-developed and intelligible design in the whole, or any part, of his composition. The beats and measures and phrases are the barley-corn, inch and ell of the musical draughtsman, and without these units of measurement and proportion, neither the vital condition of Symmetry nor the equally important condition of well-regulated Contrast could be clearly established.

The *beat* is the unit of measurement in music. The *measure* is a group of beats, — two, three, four, or more, at the option of the composer. The bounds of the measures are visibly represented (on the written or printed page) by vertical lines, called bars ; and are rendered orally recognizable (to the hearer who does not see the page) by a more or less delicate emphasis, imparted — by some means or other — to the *first* pulse or beat of each measure, as accent, simply to mark where each new group begins. Those who play or sing can imagine how vague, and even chaotic, a page of music would look if these vertical bars were omitted ; and how much more difficult it would be to read than when these (not only accustomed, but truly necessary) landmarks are present. Precisely the same unintelligible impression must be, and is, conveyed to the hearer when *his* landmarks, the accents, are not indicated with sufficient emphasis or clearness to render him sensible of the beginning of each new measure.

*   *   *

The same primary system of measurement and association which is employed in enlarging the beats to measures, is then applied to the association of the measures themselves in the next larger units of musical structure, the Motive, Phrase, Period, and so forth. Unlike the measures, which are defined by the accents at their *beginning*, these larger factors of form are defined chiefly at their *end*, by the impression of occasional periodic interruption, exactly analogous to the pauses at the end of poetic lines, or at the commas, semicolons and the like, in a prose paragraph. These interruptions of the musical current, called Cadences, are generally so well defined that even the more superficial listener is made aware of a division of the musical pattern into its sections and parts, each one of which closes as recognizably (though not as irrevocably) as the very last sentence of the piece.

Cadences serve the same purpose in music, then, as do the punctuation marks in rhetoric; and an idea of the senselessness and confusion of a musical composition, if left devoid of cadences in sufficient number and force, may be gleaned from an experimental test of the effect of a page of prose, read with persistent disregard of its commas, colons, and other marks of " cadence."

* * *

Another evidence of Form in music, that is at once subtle and powerful, rests upon what might be termed the *linear* quality of melody. The famous old definition of a line as a " succession of points," tallies so accurately with that of melody (as a " succession of single tones "), that it is not only proper, but peculiarly forceful, to speak of melodies as *tone-lines*. Our conception of a melody or tune, our ability to recognize and reproduce it, depends far more upon its undulations, its rising, falling, or resting level, than upon its rhythmic features (the varying lengths of its tones). These movements trace a resonant line before our mind's eye as surely, though perhaps not as distinctly, as the pencil of the artist traces the lines of an image upon the paper ; and this process is going on constantly, from beginning to end, in every piece of music. In a portrait it describes the contours of face and figure, — in a word, the *Form ;* in the musical composition it fulfils, to a **great** extent, the self-same mission, that of defining the Form. One clear, predominating tone-line traces the "air" or tune of the piece; and this is often the only line that arrests the hearer's attention; but there are other tone-lines, less prominent and less extended and coherent, gliding along harmoniously beside the Melody proper, which (something like the shading in a picture) contribute to the richness of the design, and perform their share in proving and illuminating the Form of the whole.

This is most salient in music for orchestra, where each player describes an individual tone-line, rendered all the more distinct and recognizable by the specific "color" of his instrument; and that is the chief, perhaps the sole, reason why the orchestra is esteemed the most complete and perfect medium of musical expression.

Unity and Variety. — As much as opinions and beliefs may differ, among music critics, as to the necessity of Form in music, and the conditions of its existence, no reasonable objection can be taken to the hypothesis that *Clearness* and *Attractiveness* are the two vital requisites upon which the enjoyment of any art depends. The artist's utterances or creations must be intelligible, and they must be interesting. The lack, partial or total, of either of these qualities neutralizes the force of the intended impression, in precise proportion to the default.

In musical composition these two requisites are embodied in the principles of Unity and Variety.

Unity — in its various technical phases of Uniformity, Regularity, Similarity, Equality, Agreement, or whatever other synonym we may find it convenient to use — is the condition out of which the composer must secure intelligibility, clearness, definiteness of expression. Glance at Ex. 2, and note the evidences of unity (similarity) in the rhythmic and melodic formation of the first four measures.

Variety — in its most comprehensive application — is the medium he must employ to arouse and sustain the hearer's interest. Glance again at Ex. 2, and note the contrast between the two halves of the first four measures, and between these and the following two measures.

These conditions are, of course, squarely opposed to each other, though their interaction is reciprocal rather than antagonistic ; and, from what has been said, it is obvious that they are of equal importance.   Hence, as was declared on the second page, the great problem of the art-creator consists in so balancing their operations that neither may encroach upon the domain of the other.   For too constant and palpable Unity will inevitably paralyze interest ; while too much Variety will as surely tend to obscure the distinctness of the design.

*   *   *

The workings of the principle of Unity (to which attention must first be given, because it appears to come first in the order of creation) are shown in the following elementary details of composition :—

(1) Music is not an art that deals with space, but with Time ; therefore the units of its metrical structure are not inches and the like, but divisions of time, the basis of which is the *beat*.   The principle of Unity dictates that the beats which are associated in one and the same musical sentence shall be of equal duration. Every musician admits the necessity of keeping "strict time" — that is, marking the beats in regular, equal pulses.   The sub-divisions of the beats (for example, the eighth or sixteenth notes within a beat) must also be symmetric.   So imperative is this law that it generally prevails through the entire piece, with only such temporary elongations or contractions (marked *ritardando* or *accelerando*) as may be introduced for oratorical effects.

(2) The beats are grouped in *measures* of uniform duration that is, containing equal numbers of beats.

(3) The natural *accent* falls upon the corresponding beat, namely, the first, of each measure ; therefore it recurs regularly, at uniform intervals of time.

(4) The *melodic contents* of the first measure, or measures, are copied (more or less literally) in the next measure, or measures ;

and are encountered again and again in the later course of the piece, thus insuring a fairly uniform melodic impression from which the character and identity of the composition are derived. Turn to the 8th Song Without Words of Mendelssohn, and observe how insistently the figure

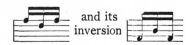

run through the whole number.

(5) The specific figure of the *accompaniment* is usually repro-duced from measure to measure (or group to group) throughout whole sections of the piece. Observe, in the 37th Song Without Words, how constantly the ascending figure of six tones recurs in the lower part (left hand). Glance also at No. 30; No. 1; No. 25. Many other evidences of Unity are invariably present in good music, so naturally and self-evidently that they almost escape our notice. Some of these are left to the student's discernment; others will engage our joint attention in due time.

*   *   *

In every one of these manifestations of unity there lies the germ of the principle of Variety, which quickens into life with the action of the former, always following, as offspring and consequence of the primary unity. Thus : —

(1) The *beats*, though uniform in duration, differ from each other in force. The first pulse in each measure (or metric group of any size) is heavier, stronger, than the following. It — the first — is the "impulse," and is what is called the accent. This dynamic distinction it is that gives rise to the two fundamental classes of rhythm, the duple and triple. In duple rhythm the accent is followed by one unaccented or lighter beat, so that regu-lar alternation of heavy and light pulses prevails incessantly. In triple rhythm the accent is followed by *two* lighter beats, creating similarly constant, but *irregular* alternation of heavy and light pulses.

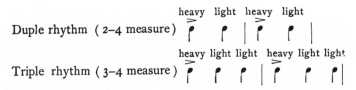

This distinction is so significant and so striking, that the music lover who is eager to gain the first clues to the structural purpose of a composition, should endeavor to recognize which one of these two rhythmic species underlies the movement to which he is listening. It is fairly certain to be one or the other continuously. Of duple measure, the march and polka are familiar examples; of triple measure, the waltz and mazurka. The "regularity" of the former rhythm imparts a certain stability and squareness to the entire piece, while triple rhythm is more graceful and circular in effect.

(2) The same dynamic distinction applies also to whole *measures*, and

(3) to *accents*. The first of two successive measures, or of two or more accents, is always a trifle heavier than the other.

(4) The *melodic contents* of the first measure may be exactly reproduced in the succeeding measure; but if this is the case, they are very unlikely to appear still again in the next (third) measure, for that would exaggerate the condition of Unity and create the effect of monotony.

The measure marked *b* is exactly like *a*. But *c* is all the more contrasting, on account of this similarity.

Or, the melodic contents of a measure may be thus reproduced, as far as the rhythm and direction of the tones are concerned, but — for variety — they may be shifted to a higher or lower place upon the staff, or may be otherwise modified.

Compare the groups marked *a* and *b*, and observe how the principles of unity and variety are both active in these four measures,
and how their effect is heightened by the formation of *c*.

(5) The figures of the accompaniment, though reproduced in uniform rhythmic values and melodic direction, undergo constant modifications in pitch and in shape, similar to those shown in Ex. 2.
See, again, No. 37 of the Songs Without Words and note the
changes in the formation of the otherwise uniform six-tone groups.

Lesson 1.—The student is to study this chapter thoroughly,
and write answers to the following questions; if possible, without
reference to the text:—

1. What does Form in music mean?
2. Define the conditions which constitute good form.
3. When is a composition faulty in form?
4. What do discriminating listeners recognize in music?
5. What is the difference between the sounds of music and those of language?
6. How does this prove the necessity of form?
7. By what is the presence of form in music shown?
8. What is the beat?
9. What is the measure?
10. By what means are the measures indicated, (1) to the reader; (2) to the
    listener?
11. To what does the further multiplication of the beats give rise?
12. What are cadences?
13. What purpose do they serve in music?
14. What is the best general name for a melody?
15. What object does it fulfil in music form?
16. What are the two vital requisites upon which the enjoyment of an art
    creation depends?
17. What purpose does Unity serve?
18. What purpose does Variety serve?
19. What is the great problem of the art-creator?
20. Define the conditions that confirm the principle of unity in music.
21. Define the evidences of variety in music.

CHAPTER II. FUNDAMENTAL DETAILS.

Time. — Time is the same thing in music that it is everywhere else in nature. It is what passes while a piece of music is being played, sung, or read. It is like the area of the surface upon which the musical structure is to be erected, and which is measured or divided into so many units for this, so many for that, so many for the other portion of the musical Form. Time is that quantity which admits of the necessary reduction to units (like the feet and inches of a yardstick), whereby a System of Measurement is established that shall determine the various lengths of the tones, define their rhythmic conditions, and govern the co-operation of several melodies sung or played together. Time is the canvas upon which the musical images are drawn — in melodic *lines*.

Tempo. — This refers to the degree of motion. The musical picture is not constant, but panoramic; we never hear a piece of music all at once, but as a panorama of successive sounds. Tempo refers to the rate of speed with which the scroll passes before our minds. Thus we speak of rapid tempo (*allegro*, and the like), or slow tempo (*adagio*), and so forth.

Beats. — The beats are the units in our System of Measurement, — as it were, the inches upon our yardstick of time; they are the particles of time that we mark when we " count," or that the conductor marks with the "beats" of his baton. Broadly speaking, the ordinary beat (in moderate tempo) is about equivalent to a second of time; to less or more than this, of course, in rapid or slow tempo. Most commonly, the beat is represented in written music by the quarter-note, as in 2–4, 3–4, 4–4, 6–4 measure. But the composer is at liberty to adopt any value he pleases (8th, 16th, half-note) as beat. In the first study in Clementi's

11

"Gradus ad Parnassum," the time-signature is 3–1, the whole note as beat ; in the 8th Song Without Words it is 6–16, the sixteenth note as beat ; in the last pianoforte sonata of Beethoven (op. 111), last movement, the time-signatures are 9–16, 6–16, and 12–32, the latter being, probably, the smallest beat ever chosen.

Measures. — A measure is a group of beats. The beats are added together, in measures, to obtain a larger unit of time, because larger divisions are more convenient for longer periods ; just as we prefer to indicate the dimensions of a house, or farm, in feet or rods, rather than in inches.

Measures differ considerably in extent in various compositions, inasmuch as the number of beats enclosed between the vertical bars may be, and is, determined quite arbitrarily. What is known as a Simple measure contains either the two beats (heavy-light) of the fundamental duple group, or the three beats (heavy-light-light) of the triple group, shown in the preceding chapter. Compound measures are such as contain more than two or three beats, and they must always be multiplications, or groups, of a Simple measure ; for whether so small as to comprise only the fundamental groups of two or three beats (as in 2–4, 3–8, 3–4 measure), or so large as to embrace as many as twelve beats or more (as in 4–4, 6–4, 6–8, 9–8, 12–8 measure), the measure represents, practically, either the duple or triple species, Simple or Compound. Thus, a measure of four beats, sometimes called (needlessly) quadruple rhythm, is merely twice two beats ; the species is actually *duple ;* the alternation of heavy and light pulses is regular ; and therefore the third beat is again an accent, as well as the first, though *less heavy.* A measure of 6–8 is triple species, with accents at beats one and four, precisely as if an additional vertical bar were inserted after the third beat. In a word, then, the size of the adopted measure is of no consequence, as long as it is retained uniformly through the section to which it belongs ; and there is no *real* difference between 2–4 and 4–4 measure, excepting in the number of bars used.

A curious and rare exception to this rule of the compound measure occurs when five or seven beats are grouped together. This involves a mingling of the duple and triple species, and, consequently, an irregular disposition of the accents; for instance, 5–4 measure is either 3 + 2 or 2 + 3 beats, with corresponding accentuation:

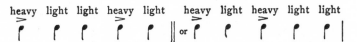

heavy light light heavy light   heavy light heavy light light

Rhythm. — This word signifies arrangement, — a principle applied, in music, to the distribution or arrangement of the tones according to their various *time-values*. The system of measurement (or metric system) furnishes tone material with all the details of division, proportion and comparison; but this, alone, is not rhythm. The metric system affords the basis for rational and definable rhythm, but "rhythm" itself does not enter into the proposition until differentiated factors are associated and opposed to each other.

Ex. 3. etc.

The first measure of this hymn is, by itself, merely an exponent of the metric principle, for it consists of three uniform quarter-notes. The second measure, however, is a rhythmic one, because, by dotting the first of the three beats, three different time-values are obtained (dotted quarter, eighth, and quarter). Further, by association and comparison with each other, both measures assume a collective rhythmic significance.

The rhythmic disposition of the tones is to a certain extent optional with the composer, but by no means wholly so; the rules of rhythm are probably the most definite and obvious of all the rules of music writing. They do not concern the analytical student intimately, but at least the general distinction between regular and irregular rhythm should be understood: — We have seen that the natural accent (the "heavy" pulse) is invariably repre-sented by the first beat of a rhythmic group; and that one or two lighter pulses intervene before the next accent appears. Further, it is self-evident that the rhythmic weight of a tone is proportionate to its length, or time-value; longer tones produce heavier, and shorter tones lighter, impressions. The deduction from these two facts is, then, that the rhythmic arrangement is *regular* when the comparatively longer tones occupy the accented beats, or the accented fractions of the beats; and *irregular* when shorter tones occupy the accents, or when longer tones are shifted to any com-paratively lighter pulse of the measure or group.

The rhythm of the second measure in Ex. 3 is regular, be-cause the longest tone stands at the beginning of the measure, thus confirming (and, in fact, creating) the accent. The rhythm in Ex. 1 is also regular, throughout, the light eighth-notes oc-cupying the light third beat, and the heavy dotted-quarter the heavy pulse (in the third measure). Ex. 2 is strikingly definite in rhythm, because the time-values are so greatly diversified; and the arrangement is regular.

On the other hand, the following is an example of irregular rhythm:

BEETHOVEN.

Ex. 4.

The longer (heavier) tones are placed in the middle of the measure, between the beats; the tie at the end of measure 3 places the heavy note at the end, instead of the beginning, of the measure, and cancels the accent of the fourth measure. These irregular forms of rhythm are called syncopation. See also Ex. 6, second Phrase.

Melody. — Any succession of *single* tones is a melody. If we strike the keys of the piano with two or more fingers of each hand simultaneously, we produce a body of tones, which — if they are so chosen that they blend harmoniously — is called a Chord ; and a series of such chords is an illustration of what is known as Harmony. If, however, we play with one finger only, we produce a melody. The human voice, the flute, horn, — all instruments capable of emitting but one tone at a time, — produce melody.

Melody constitutes, then, *a line of tones.* If, as we have said, Time is the canvas upon which the musical images are thrown, Melodies are the lines which trace the design or form of these images. This indicates the extreme importance of the melodic idea in music form. Without such "tone-lines" the effect would be similar to that of daubs or masses of color without a drawing, without the evidence of contour and shape.

A *good* melody, that is, a melody that appeals to the intelligent music lover as tuneful, pleasing, and intelligible, is one in which, first of all, each successive tone and each successive group of tones stands in a rational harmonic relation to the one before it, and even, usually, to several preceding tones or groups. In other words, the tones are not arranged haphazard, but with reference to their harmonious agreement with each other. For a model of good melody, examine the very first sentence in the book of Beethoven's pianoforte sonatas : —

The tones bracketed *a,* if struck all together, unite and blend in one harmonious body, so complete is the harmonic agreement of each succeeding tone with its fellows ; the same is true of the group marked *c.* The tones bracketed *b* and *d* do not admit of being struck simultaneously, it is true, but they are all parts of the same key (F minor), and are closely and smoothly connected ;

hence their concurrence, though not one of harmony (chord), is one of intimate tone relation and proximity.   Further, the whole group marked 2 corresponds in its linear formation, its rising, poising and curling, exactly to the preceding group, marked 1. This, then, is a *good* melody, — tuneful, interesting, intelligible, striking and absolutely definite.

In the second place, the tones and groups in a good melody are measured with reference to harmony of time-values ; that is, their metric condition, and their rhythmic arrangement, corroborate the natural laws already defined: — uniformity of fundamental pulse, uniform recurrence of accent, and sufficient regularity of rhythmic figure to insure a distinct and comprehensible total impression.   This also may be verified in the time-values of Ex. 5. Scrutinize also, the melodic and rhythmic conditions of Exs. 1 and 2, — and the examples on later pages, — and endeavor to vindicate their classification as "good" melodies.   Ex. 4, though an exposition of irregular rhythm, is none the less excellent on that account ; on the contrary, this irregularity, because wisely balanced by sufficient evidence of harmonious and logical agreement, only heightens the beauty and effectiveness of the melody.

*   *   *

Whenever whole bodies of tone are played successively, a number of melody lines are being described, — as many, in fact, as there are tones in each body.   For example, in playing a hymn-tune we describe (on the keyboard) the four separate melodies known as the soprano, alto, tenor and bass voices.   In a duet, unaccompanied, there are two melodic lines ; if accompanied, other melodic lines are added to these.   Thus we recognize the same system of associated lines in music as in architecture or drawing. Very rarely indeed does one single unbroken line portray a complete image.

But in music, as in drawing, the lines differ in their degrees of importance and prominence ; and, very commonly, one line overshadows all, or nearly all the rest.   This strongest tone-line is therefore apt to be designated, somewhat unfairly, *the* melody (the "tune" or "air" is more just). But, at all events, *this predominating melodic line is the most important factor of the form, the one upon which the definition and recognition of the "form" depend;* and it is therefore necessary that the student learn to distinguish it, to acquire the habit of centring his attention upon it, — in reading, listening to, or analyzing music ; and, in playing, to give it the emphasis it requires.

The importance of a tone-line depends solely upon .its conspicuousness. The principal melody — *the* Melody — is the one which is most salient, which most attracts the hearer's attention. For this reason the composer is induced to place his chief melody *above the rest of the tone-lines, because the uppermost tone strikes the ear more acutely than the lower ones,* and therefore the succession of highest tones constitutes a conspicuous line that attracts and impresses the sense most keenly.

Here then, at the top of the harmonic tone-complex, we look for the chief melody ; and here it will be found, — excepting when arbitrary emphasis (by accentuation) is imparted to some lower tone-line, so that it, for the time being, assumes a prominence equal, or superior, to that of the uppermost line. (This divided prominence is seen in the 18th Song Without Words — the *duet.*)

Lesson 2. — Write careful and complete answers to the following questions : —

1. What is Time, as applied to music?
2. What is *tempo ?*
3. Give a full definition of the beat.
4. By what time-value is it most commonly indicated ?
5. Give a full definition of the measure.
6. Why do measures differ in size?
7. What is a simple measure?
8. What is a compound measure?
9. Define duple and triple rhythms. (See also Chap. I.)
10. What does the term rhythm signify?
11. How is it applied in music?
12. When is the rhythm regular?

13. When is the rhythm irregular?
14. Define the difference between melody and harmony.
15. Give a full definition of melody.
16. What are the conditions of a good melody?
17. In what respect does music resemble architecture or drawing?
18. Are the tone-lines in a composition of equal importance?
19. What significance is to be attached to the principal tone-line?
20. Upon what does the importance of a tone-line depend?
21. Where is the chief melody usually placed?

CHAPTER III. FIGURE AND MOTIVE.

The Melodic Figure. — The smallest unit in musical composition is the single tone. The smallest cluster of successive tones
(from two to four or five in number) that will convey a definite
musical impression, as miniature musical idea, is called a Figure.
Assuming the single tone to represent the same unit of expression
as a letter of the alphabet, the melodic figure would be defined as
the equivalent of a complete (small) word ; — pursuing the comparison further, a series of figures constitutes the melodic Motive,
equivalent to the smallest group of words (a subject with its article
and adjective, for example) ; and two or three motives make a
Phrase, equivalent to the complete, though comparatively brief,
sentence (subject, predicate, and object). This definition, amply
illustrated in the following examples, serves also to point out the
significant resemblance between the structure of language and of
music. The principal melody is, as it were, the voice of the
speaker, whose message is framed wholly out of the primary tones,
or letters of the musical alphabet. The association of primary
tone-units, in successive order, results first in the figure, then in
the motive, then the phrase, period, and so forth, in the manner
of natural growth, till the narrative is ended. The following example, though extending beyond our present point of observation,
is given as an illustration of this accumulative process (up to the
so-called Period) : —

The tones bracketed *a* are the Figures ; two (in the last measures, three) of these are seen to form Motives ; two of these motives make the Phrase ; and the whole sentence, of two phrases, is a Period.   See also Ex. 1 and Ex. 2, in which the formation of figures is very distinct.

The pregnancy and significance of each of these tiny musical " words " (or figures, as we are to call them),— small and apparently imperfect as they are, — can best be tested by concentrating the attention upon each as if it stood alone upon the page; it is such vitality of the separate particles that invests a musical masterwork with its power and permanency of interest.

*   *   *

Defining the Figures. — It is not always easy to distinguish the figures in a melodic sentence.   While they are unquestionably analogous to the words in speech, they are by no means as concrete, nor are they separated as distinctly, as the words upon a written or printed sheet.   This is in keeping with the intangible quality of music, and the peculiar vagueness of its medium of expression ; the quality which veils its intrinsic purport from the mass of music admirers, and lends it such exquisite and inexplicable charm to all hearers alike.

In a word, it is not the common practice for a composer to cut up his melodic sentences into separately recognizable small particles, by distinctly marking each component *figure*.   Here and there it is done, by way of contrast, or emphasis, or for a definite rhythmic effect, — as shown in Ex. 2 and Ex. 6.   But more generally the figures are so closely interlinked that the whole sentence may impress the hearer as one coherent strain, with an occasional interruption. The very minute "breaks" between figures are often nearly or quite imperceptible; and in many cases it is possible to define the figures of a motive in various, equally plausible ways, simply because the "breaks" (which are of course surely present, and become more and more apparent between the larger members of a composition) are likely to be too inconsiderable among these smallest factors of the melodic form.

The following three guides may serve to indicate the extremities of the melodic figures : —

(1) A brief rest, or a longer tone, usually marks the end of a figure. This is fully illustrated in Ex. 6. See also Ex. 10, Ex. 12.

(2) Similarity of formation (rhythm and melodic direction) almost invariably defines the mutually opposed, and therefore separable, divisions of the melody, — both small and large. For example (the figures are bracketed *a*) : —

See also Ex. 1. The operation of this exceedingly important rule of "corresponding formation" (about which more will be said later on) is seen — on a larger scale — in Ex. 2, Ex. 5, and Ex. 6, where it defines the whole *motive*.

(3) In default of more definite signs, the figures may be found to correspond to the metric groups (that is, in lengths of whole or half measures). Thus : —

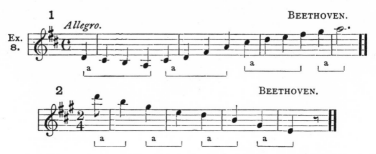

This example illustrates the interlinking of the figures, and suggests the difficulty that may be encountered in the effort to define melodic figures. The difficulty is probably greatest in melodies of a lyric character, where it is necessary to sustain the coherency of the sentence ; for instance, in many of the Songs Without Words, — see No. 40, No. 22, and others, in which an entirely definite separation of the figures is well-nigh a hopeless task

For this reason, — that is, because the melodic divisions are so minute and vague between these smaller particles of the musical sentence, — it is advisable *to give no heed to any factor smaller than the " motive,"* and to undertake the analysis of nothing less than the latter ; for even the most scrupulous " phrasing," in the playing of a composition, must avoid the risk of incoherency, almost certain to result from distinctly separating all the figures. The melodies in Ex. 8 should not betray the secret of their formation.

The Melodic Motive or Phrase-member. — This, as has already been stated, is a somewhat longer section, compounded of two or more figures. Being thus longer, the " breaks " or spaces between motives are generally more emphatic and recognizable than those between the figures, and therefore it is easier, as a rule, to define the extremities of motives.

Melodic motives differ in length from one to four measures; by
far the most common extent, however, is two measures, and the
student will do wisely to accept this dimension and analyze accord-
ingly, unless there is unmistakable evidence to the contrary.   The
indications are precisely the same as those illustrated in the preceding two examples as guides for the definition of figures.

For example: —

In the first of these examples the extent of the motives is
proven by each of the three given guides: the rest, which marks
the end of the first member; the similarity of melodic and rhythmic formation, which proclaims the beginning of the second
member, parallel with that of the first; and the regular (two-
measure) dimension.   In Nos. 2 and 3 there are no rests between
the motives, and the melodic formation differs; here it is the
standard of two measures that defines the members.

Ex. 3 is a two-measure motive.   In Exs. 2, 5, and 6, the motives
are all two measures in length.

In the following: —

one is tempted to call each *single* measure a motive, because of the number of tones it contains, and the weight (length) of the final tone, which makes a much more emphatic interruption than commonly occurs between figures.

And in the following, on the other hand: —

the entire four-measure sentence is evidently one motive, for there is no recognizable indication of an interruption at any point. The same is true of the two melodies given in Ex. 8.

The following illustrates an irregular (uneven) association of members: —

Here again, there may be a disposition to adopt the upper line of brackets, assigning a single measure to each motive. But both her♭, *and in Ex. 10,* the student is advised to adhere to the two-measure standard ; he will avoid much needless confusion by so doing, — at least until he shall have so developed and sharpened his sense of melodic syntax that he can apprehend the finer shades of distinction in the " motion and repose " of a melody. Adopting the lower line of brackets, we discover successive members of unequal length, the first one containing two, the next one three measures.

Preliminary Tones. — It is a singularly effective and pregnant quality of the element of musical rhythm, that its operations are not bounded by the vertical bars which mark off the measures. That is to say, a rhythmic figure (and, in consequence, a melodic figure or motive) does not necessarily extend from bar to bar, but may run from the middle (or any other point) of one measure, to the middle (or corresponding point) of the next ; precisely as prosodic rhythm comprises poetic feet which begin either with an accented or with an unaccented syllable. See Ex. 10. Hence the significant rule, *that a melodic member may begin at any part of a measure,* upon an accented or an unaccented beat, or upon any fraction of a beat. For example : —

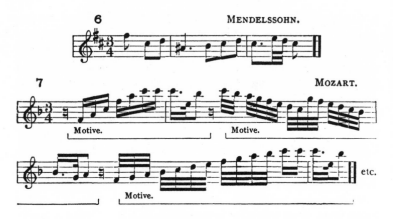

In No. 1, the motive begins squarely with the measure, upon the accented beat. In No. 2, the same motive is enlarged by two tones at the outset, which locates its beginning upon the fourth 8th — the second half of the second beat. In No. 3 the motive begins upon an accented beat, but it is the lighter (secondary) accent of the 3d beat. The various conditions of unaccented beginnings in Nos. 4, 5 and 6 are easily recognizable. In No. 7 quite a large fraction of a measure precedes the first accent (at the beginning of the full measure). Examine, also, all the preceding examples, and note the different accented or unaccented locations of the first tone, in each figure and motive.

When a figure or motive starts at the accented beat, it begins, so to speak, in the right place ; *any tone or tones which precede the accent are merely preliminary or introductory tones.* While they are very desirable and necessary, in the fulfilment of certain purposes, they are not an *essential* part of the motive ; they appear to represent the ornamental rather than the stable element of the melodic sentence, and their employment is therefore a matter of option and taste rather than of absolute necessity. The accent indicates the point where the body of the motive begins ; the accent is the point where the stake is driven ; all that goes before is simply preparatory, — the changeable material which flutters about the fixed center. Therefore the preliminary tones do not indicate the *essential* or actual beginning of the motive, but its apparent or conditional beginning only ; or what might be called its *melodic* beginning. For this reason, also, the actual "first measure" of a motive or phrase or sentence of any kind is always the first FULL measure, — the measure which contains the first primary accent ; that is to say, the preliminary tone or tones do not count as first measure For this reason, further, it is evident that preliminary tones are invariably to be regarded as borrowed from the final measure of the preceding motive or phrase ; they must be accounted for in some way, — must derive their metric pulse from some group, — and as they cannot be a part of the first measure, they obviously form a borrowed portion of the (preceding) last measure.   This will be better understood by reference to Ex. 14, No. 3 ; the two 16ths at the end of the 4th measure (preliminary tones of the following phrase) are borrowed from the *f* which precedes, — the final tone of the first phrase, that would, but for this reduction, have been the full half-note necessary to complete the four measures (like the final *g*).

Perhaps the most striking feature of this rule of preliminary tones is the absolute freedom of its application.   It is *always* wholly optional with the composer to begin his figure or motive at whatever part of the measure he may elect ; at the accent or not ; with or without preliminary tones ; to borrow beats from the preceding ending or not, as his judgment or taste, or possibly some indirect requirement, may decide.   So valid is this license, that it is by no means unusual to find consecutive members of the same phrase beginning at different points in the measure.   This results, apparently, in motives of irregular, unsymmetric lengths ; but no confusion is possible if the student will recollect and apply the rule that the objective point (the heart, so to speak) of each motive is the first primary accent it contains ; counting from these points, all irregularities of melodic extent become purely accidental

and harmless.   For illustration (tne preliminary tones are marked
a) : —

In No. 1, the first motive evidently ends with the longer tone,
g-sharp.   In No. 2, each one of the four motives differs from the
others in length ; the sum of them is, however, exactly 24 beats,
or 8 measures ; hence, each one is *actually* a two-measure motive,
counting from accent to accent.   The upper numbers indicate the
actual, vital beginning of each motive.

This very natural, and fairly common, inequality increases the
difficulty of analysis somewhat.   A knowledge of the principal

chords, and familiarity with their manner of employment in composition, greatly facilitates the task, because the harmonic design furnishes in many cases the only unmistakable clue to the extremities of the melodic members. The difficulty finally vanishes only when the student has learned to appreciate the declamatory quality of all good melody, and can detect its inflections, its pauses; can *feel* which (and how many) of its tones are coherent and inseparable, and where the points of repose interrupt the current, and thus divulge the sense of the melodic sentence.

Lesson 3. — Analyze the third Song Without Words of Mendelssohn (A major, the so-called Hunting Song); first of all, locate the principal melody, — it is not always the uppermost line of tones; then divide this melody into its melodic motives, marking the "breaks" which separate each from the following one; the figures may be noted. also, but only mentally. No. 35 may also be analyzed in the same manner.

CHAPTER IV. THE PHRASE.

The Phrase. — It is not altogether easy to give a precise defini-tion of the phrase. Like so many of the factors which enter into the composition of this most abstract, ideal, and intangible of the arts, the phrase demands considerable latitude of treatment, and will not readily submit to strict limitations or absolute technical conditions. Perhaps the most correct definition is, that the term phrase is equivalent to "sentence," and represents the smallest musical section that expresses a *complete* idea; not necessarily wholly finished, and therefore independent of other adjoining phrases, but at least as complete *in itself* as is an ordinary brief sentence in grammar, with its subject, predicate, and object. It should be sufficiently long to establish the sense of tonality, the consciousness of beginning, course, and ending, and should exhibit a certain (though limited) amount of palpable and satisfying melodic and harmonic contents. For this reason, the Phrase, and nothing smaller, should be regarded as the structural basis of musical form.

The factors defined in the preceding chapter (the figure and motive) are, as a rule, decidedly less than is demanded of a complete phrase, which — as has been intimated — usually con-sists in the union of two (possibly more) motives, — just as the motive is compounded of figures, and the latter of single tones.

In some, comparatively rare, cases the composer gives a phrase an independent place upon his page, as complete miniature sen-tence, not directly connected with other phrases. This may be seen, very plainly, at the beginning (the first four or five measures) of the Songs Without Words, Nos. 28, 41, 35, 3, 4, 16. Examine each, carefully, and the nature of the phrase in its most definite form will become apparent.

Such independent phrases are most likely to be found, like the above, at the beginning or end of a larger composition, to which they are related indirectly, as isolated introduction, or postlude. Thus, the following complete phrase appears at the beginning of a song :

Its division into two melodic motives, and the subdivision of these into figures, is plainly marked.

When the phrase assumes such a conspicuous position, and is so complete and definite in its effect as the ones just seen, there is naturally no difficulty in recognizing and defining its extremities. But the task of phrase analysis is by no means always thus easy.

Length of the Regular Phrase. — Fortunately for the work of analysis, there are certain established landmarks of forms, so conscientiously observed, and so firmly grounded in the practices of classic writing (because the necessary consequences of natural law), that it is generally practicable to fix fairly regular and plausible boundaries to the phrase, notwithstanding the freedom and elasticity which characterize the application of the syntactic principle in music.

Therefore the student will find that a phrase, in the great majority of cases, covers exactly *four measures,* and will seldom be misled if he looks for the end of his phrase four measures beyond its beginning. This refers, be it understood, only to measures of average size (in the ordinary time denominations, 3-4, 4-4, 6-8 measure). If the measures are uncommonly large (9-8, 12-8), the phrase will probably cover no more than two of them ; or, if small (2–4, or 3–4 in rapid tempo), the phrase may extend to the eighth measure. The operation of this four-measure rule is exhibited with striking regularity and persistence in the *Jugend Album* of Schumann (op. 68); throughout its forty-three numbers there are probably no more than a half-dozen phrases whose length differs from this standard. For example:

SCHUMANN, Op. 68, No. 11.

It will be observed that the first (and also the third) of these phrases consists of two exactly similar two-measure motives. This seems to lend some confirmation to the idea of a two-measure phrase; but the student is warned against deviating from his four-measure standard, upon such evidence as this. Many instances will be found, like these, in which the impression of a complete phrase is not gained until the motive of two measures has been thus repeated ; *the repetition is necessary*, in order to finish the sentence, and this proves that the two measures alone do not constitute the " complete idea" which we expect the phrase to represent.

The same regularity of dimension will usually be found in all kinds of dance music ; in technical exercises (for instance, the études of Czerny and others) ; and in all music of a simple or popular character.

*   *   *

Exceptions. — In its ordinary, normal condition the phrase is a musical sentence four measures in length. But this rule has its necessary exceptions ; necessary because, as we have learned, the principle of Variety is quite as vital as that of Unity or symmetry. The phrase is not always regular ; by various means and for various reasons, it occasionally assumes an irregular form. When such irregular phrases are encountered (phrases of less or more than four measures) the student will best distinguish them by defining their extremities, their beginning and ending — as " beginning " and "ending," without reference to their length. This should not be attended with any serious difficulty ; at least not to the observant student who reads his musical page thoughtfully, and attaches some meaning to the figures and motives of the melody ; who endeavors to recognize the extent to which the successive tones appear to cling together (like the letters in a word) and constitute an unbroken melodic number, — and, in so doing, also recognizes the points where this continuity is broken, and a new number is announced. Much assistance may be derived from the fact — striking in its simplicity — that the ending of one phrase defines, at the same time, the beginning of the next, and *vice versa.* The locating of one, therefore. serves to locate the other. There is, usually, something sufficiently indicative about a " beginning," to

render it noticeable to a careful observer, and the same is true of
an "ending." This is illustrated in the following:

No. 1 is from the pianoforte sonata, op. 10, No. 3, second
movement; see the original. This phrase exhibits an ending, unmistakably, in the *fifth* measure, and not in the fourth. Its form
is therefore irregular.

In No. 2 (from the first pianoforte sonata), the first phrase ends
with the fourth measure, obviously, for the evidence of a new

" beginning " in the following measure is perfectly clear ; the phrase
is therefore regular. But the next phrase runs on to the *sixth*
measure from this point (the tenth from the beginning of the
whole), because there is no earlier evidence of an " ending."
Observe that the first phrase has a preliminary quarter-note, the
second phrase none. Turning to Mendelssohn's Songs Without
Words, the very first (introductory) phrase of No. 3 is five measures in length ; the first one in No. 35 also contains five measures ;
the first one in No. 16, and in No. 9, contains three measures.
The irregular phrase will be again considered (in a different aspect)
in a later chapter.

The recognition of these syntactic traits of the melodic sentence is of great moment to the player, for they constitute the information upon which conscious, intelligent, effective *phrasing*
depends ; and without intelligent phrasing, without a clear exposition of the formation and arrangement of the members and phrases,
full comprehension and adequate enjoyment of a musical composition is impossible.

*   *   *

Contents of the Phrase. — The question may arise, what is it
that makes a phrase, — the rhythm, harmony, or melody ? Strictly
speaking, all three ; for music subsists in the ceaseless co-operation
of these three primary elements of composition, and no phrase is
wholly complete without the evidence of each and all. Generaliz-
ing the definitions already given, the function of each of these
primary elements may be thus described : The element of harmony
regulates the choice of the tones that are to sound together ; the
upright shafts of tone (chords) which determine the *body*, or frame-
work, of the music. The element of melody regulates the choice
of single tones, selected from the successive shafts of harmony,
that are to form a connected line or strand of tones (in horizontal
order, so to speak), — something like a chain or chains stretched
from harmonic post to post, which describe the figure or *outline* of
the musical image. The element of rhythm gives the whole body

its *life*, — regulates the choice of varying lengths, defining the infinitely varied " tapping " of the musical mechanism.

It is evident, from this, that no vivid, satisfying musical im pression can be created in the absence of any one of these essential elements.　But, for all that, they are not of equal importance; and, in determining the extremities of the phrase (and of all other factors of musical structure), the melody takes precedence over harmony and rhythm.　That is to say, that in his analysis of figures, motives, phrases, periods, and so forth, the student's attention should be centered upon the melody, — that chain of successive single tones which, as repeatedly stated, usually describes the *uppermost* line of the harmonic and rhythmic body.　That is the reason why the illustrations given in this book are so frequently limited to the melody alone; it is the pencil point which traces the design, describes the form, of the musical composition.

Lesson 4. — Procure the *Jugend Album*, op. 68, of Schumann, and mark the phrases in Nos. 1, 2, 4, 5, 6, 7, 8, 9, 13, 18, 20, and others.　In the given numbers the phrases are all regular, — four measures in length.

Analyze in the same manner Mendelssohn's Songs Without Words, Nos. 27, 22 (first phrase, five measures), 48, 28, 35, and others; occasional irregularities may be encountered.

Also Beethoven, pianoforte sonata; op. 14, No. 2, second movement (C major, *andante*); and op. 26, first movement.

A few cautious experiments may also be made in analyzing any composition which the student may chance to be studying, especially if not too elaborate.　The necessary safeguard consists in simply passing over every confusing point, limiting the analysis to those phrases that are self defining, for the present, — until greater experience and fuller information shall have been gained.

CHAPTER V.   CADENCES.

Cadences in General. — A cadence is the ending of a phrase.

Strictly speaking, every interruption or "break" between figures, and between all melodic members, is a cadence; but the term "cadence" is applied to nothing smaller than entire phrases.

The cadence is the point of Repose which creates the necessary contrast with the condition of Action that prevails more or less constantly during the phrase ; and the effect of this point of repose is, therefore, to separate one phrase from the next. The cadential effect is generally produced by two or three chords, the last one of which is called the cadence-chord, and stands, when the cadence is perfectly regular, upon an accented beat of the final measure.   This, according to our definition of the phrase, will most commonly be the fourth measure.

For example :

The first chord in the fourth measure, on the accented beat, is the "cadence-chord" ; but the preceding chord (and possibly the one before that, also) is naturally inseparable from the final one, and therefore the entire cadence would be defined technically as embracing both (or all three) of these chords.   The effect of repose is obtained *by the length of the final chord,* which exceeds that of any other melody tone in the phrase ; its time-value is a dotted quarter, because of the preliminary tone (*e*, before the first accent) which, in the original (op. 68, No. 28), precedes the next phrase in exactly the same manner.

Illustrations of the regular cadence will be found, also, in Ex. 15 and Ex. 16 ; in the latter, — consisting as it does of four consecutive phrases, four cadences occur, distinctly marked by the *longer tone* on the accented beat of each successive fourth measure.

Modification or Disguising of the Cadence. — The most natural and characteristic indication of a cadence is the *longer tone*, seen in the examples to which reference has just been made ; for a tone of greater length than its fellows is, in itself, the most conclusive evidence of a point of repose, as compared with the shorter tones in the course of the sentence, whose more prompt succession indicates the action of the phrase. (See Ex. 29.)

From this the student is not to conclude that every long tone marks a cadence. The rhythmic design of a melody is obtained by a constant interchange of long and short tones, without direct reference to the cadence alone ; and numerous examples will be found in which tones of equal, or even greater, length than the cadence-tone occur in the course of the phrase. We have already seen that the end of a motive, or even of a figure, may be marked by a longer tone, or its equivalent in rests ; and have been taught to expect a cadence in the fourth measure only, as a rule.

But the direct evidence of a cadence afforded by a longer tone is considered not only unnecessary, but in many cases distinctly undesirable. While cadences are indispensable, in music of clearly recognizable form, it is equally true that they must not be so emphatic as to check the current of melody and harmony too frequently or completely, or destroy the continuity and coherence of the members. And it is therefore an almost invariable practice, especially in music of a higher order, to modify and disguise the cadences by some means or other ; that is, to diminish the weight of the characteristic "longer tone," — to counteract, partially or entirely, the impression of actual cadential cessation, by continuing (instead of interrupting) the rhythmic pulse. This is so very common, and so confusing a device, that the effect of the various methods employed to conceal or disguise a cadence must be thoroughly understood.

It is necessary to remember, always, the rule that governs the actual body of the phrase, and its possible preliminary tones; namely, that the vital, essential starting-point of a phrase (and other factors of musical form) is *the first primary accent,* the first beat of the first *full* measure. The length of the phrase is reckoned from this point, and consequently, the cadence-chord is entitled to all the beats that remain, from its accent to the very end of the final measure. For example:

In this case the cadence-chord is not modified or disguised in the least, but takes full advantage of the six beats that make the sum of the fourth measure.

This important fact concerning the actual value of the cadence-chord remains unchanged, through all the licenses taken in disguising or (apparently) diminishing its value. Whatever means may be resorted to, in modifying the cadence, they do not alter the fact that *the cadence-chord is always entitled to this full sum of beats;* and these beats virtually represent the cadence-chord, either in its unchanged form (as in Ex. 19 and Ex. 16) or in any of the manifold disguised forms illustrated in the following examples.

One of the simplest forms is shown in Ex. 15 : — The cadence-chord, on the accented beat of the fourth measure, is entitled to the six beats contained in that final measure. One beat is borrowed for the preliminary tone of the next phrase (that does not appear in our example, but corresponds to the preliminary tone at the beginning); and three beats are represented by rests, which cancel the resonance of the melody-tone *g*, but do not actually negate the effect of the cadence-chord. In consequence of these two reductions, the time-value of the *cadence-tone* is diminished to two beats, and the whole cadence assumes a lighter, less obstinate and stagnant character. Of the six beats belonging to the cadence-chord, four are occupied by the tones of the accompaniment, which thus serves to bridge over the measure of repose without destroying the impression of a cadence.

The treatment of the cadence is similar to this in Ex. 18.

In Ex. 17, No. 1, the cadence-chord falls, properly, upon the primary accent (first beat) of the final measure — in this instance the fifth measure, as we have learned. The six beats to which it is entitled are all occupied by the simple reiteration of the final melody tone, while the sense of "interruption" is imparted by the long rest in the lower parts.

It is by thus sustaining the rhythmic pulse, during the measure allotted to the cadence-chord, that the desired dual impression, — that of cadential interruption without actual cessation, — is secured. It is like rounding off a corner that might otherwise be too angular or abrupt.

*　　*　　*

The question naturally arises: What tones are chosen to provide material for this continuation of the rhythm? They are usually derived from the cadence-chord, or its auxiliary embellishments ; and the methods employed may be classified as follows :

(1) The rhythmic pulse is marked in the accompanying (subordinate) parts, as seen in Ex. 15, Ex. 18, and the following : —

MENDELSSOHN (37)

4-measure phrase.

Ex. 20.

Cadence-chord.

The point of repose is marked by the longer melody tone *f*, on the accent of the fourth measure. The value of the cadence-chord is recorded, however, in the living tones of the accompanying figure, which here (as in almost every similar case in composition) continues its rhythmic movement undisturbed.

(2) The cadence-chord, or, more properly, the *cadence-tone* in the melody, is shifted to some later beat in the cadence measure. Thus:

MOZART.

Ex. 21.

Cadence-measure.

In this example there is in reality no irregularity, because the cadence-tone rests upon an *accented beat* (the fourth, in 6–8 measure), and the conditions of a cadence are fulfilled by *any* accent, primary or secondary, of the final measure. But it belongs, nevertheless, to this class of disguised cadences; for whatever results, thus, in abbreviating the value of the cadence-chord, lightens the effect of the cadence, and serves the desirable purpose so persistently pursued by all good writers. Further: —

BEETHOVEN.

Ex. 22.

Cadence-measure.

Nos. 2 and 3 illustrate the method most commonly adopted in shifting the cadence-tone forward to a later beat; namely, by placing an embellishing tone (usually the upper or lower neighbor) of the cadence-tone upon the accented beat belonging properly to the latter. Nos. 4 and 5 are both extreme cases; the actual cadence-tone is shifted to the very end of the measure, so that the effect of cadential interruption is very vague and transient, — and will be quite lost unless the player is intelligent enough to emphasize, slightly, the phrasing (by making a distinct, though very brief, pause before attacking the following measure). See also Ex. 17, No. 2, the first phrase; here, again, the melody runs on (through tones which embellish the cadence-chord, *f-a-c*) to the last 8th-note of the fourth measure.

(3) A certain — entirely optional — number of tones are borrowed from the value of the cadence-chord, as *preliminary tones* of the following phrase. An illustration of this has already been seen in Ex. 14, No. 2 and No. 3. It is the employment of such preliminary tones, that, as thoroughly explained in Chapter III, creates a distinction between the *melodic* beginning and the actual vital starting point of the phrase; or that gives the phrase an apparently shifted location in its measures.

Further (the actual cadence-tone is marked *) : —

No. 1 illustrates, again, the absence of preliminary tones in one phrase, and their presence in the next. In each of these examples (excepting, perhaps, No. 2) the cadence is so thoroughly disguised that there is little, if any, evidence left of the "point of repose." In No. 4, particularly, the cadence-measure is rhythmically the most active one in the phrase. And yet the presence of a genuine cadence at each of these places, marked *, is as certain and indisputable as in Ex. 19. The ear will accept a cadence upon the slightest evidence *in the right place,* — where a cadence is expected. See, also, Mozart pianoforte sonata No. 10 (in D major), first 12 measures ; measure 8 is a *cadence-measure.*

Here follow a few more examples which illustrate the most extreme application of this principle of borrowed tones, — a mode of treatment very common in the music of Mozart, Haydn, and, in fact, all classic writers : —

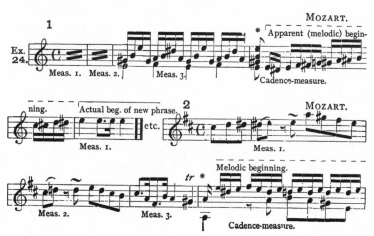

Meas. 1.   Meas. 1.   BEETHOVEN.   Meas. 2.

Melodic beginning.

Meas. 3.   Cadence-measure.

It is difficult to believe that in each of these cases the long array of 16th-notes should not constitute the actual beginning of the phrase, but are only preliminary; and yet this is the only correct view to take of it, and it is the view which will simplify all analysis, when thoroughly comprehended. It must be seen that the cluster of 16th-notes in the cadence-measure (of the preceding phrase) is *one-sixteenth short of a full measure,* and, therefore, it does not represent the first measure of the next phrase, because our inviolable rule is that the first measure of a phrase is its first *full* measure. The above examples emphasize the correct manner of counting the measures; and they simply illustrate possible methods of *disguising the cadence.*

In some cases it is difficult to determine whether the tones which thus disturb the "repose" of the cadence-measure belong to the cadence-chord (that is, to the *present* phrase), or, as preliminary tones, to the following phrase. Upon careful scrutiny, however, it will be found possible to decide, by examining their melodic bearing, to which phrase they pertain. In Example 22, they are manifestly (even in No. 5) a part of the present phrase; in Example 23 and 24 they are as certainly preliminary to the phrase which follows. In the following example they seem to constitute an entirely independent little "interlude," without direct reference to either phrase:

* * *

The Elision. — Finally, there are some (very rare) instances where the composer appears to yield to the seductive influence of such extensive preliminary groups as those seen in Example 24, and by setting aside the trifling discrepancy, permits the apparent preliminary tones to represent the *actual first measure of the next phrase.* This is easily accomplished, when, as in Example 24, No. 2, it is only one 16th-note short of a full measure. And although this 16th, being the cadence-chord, is actually equivalent to the whole measure, it is sometimes less confusing to the hearer to silence it. This is called stifling the cadence (or Elision); and its presence depends simply upon sufficient proof that what was supposed to be the cadence-measure (and to a certain extent *is* such) is at the same time *really the first measure of the next sentence.* The following contains an illustration of the elision of a cadence:

The proofs of this very singular and apparently untrustworthy analysis are: ① That there is absolutely no doubt about the first cadence, marked *; ② that a cadence is consequently due, and expected, four measures later, — this proving the measure in question to be the "cadence-measure of the old phrase," as it is marked and as it appeals to our sense of cadence; "③ that the last four measures unmistakably represent a regular, compact phrase, — this proving that the "cadence-measure of the old phrase" is unquestionably *at the same time the first measure, or actual beginning, of the new phrase.* In a word, one measure is lost — not in effect, for the elements of the expected cadence are all present, — but in the counting. This lost measure is the stifled cadence-measure, omitted by Elision.

Such cases are, as stated, very rare; so rare that the student will do wisely to leave them quite out of his calculations.

In order to elucidate the embarrassing matter still more fully, we shall take two more examples of a very misleading character, which the superficial observer would probably define as elisions, but which are almost certainly regular cases of disguised cadence merely :

Here again there is no doubt of the presence of a cadence at the first * ; but this "cadence-measure" appears almost as certainly to be at the same time the initial measure of a new phrase. This, however, proves not to be the case, because *there are four measures left, without this one.* That is, counting backward from the final cadence, we locate the "first measure" after, not *with,*

the cadence-measure.   And this is the way the passage was meant
to sound by its author, and the way it will and must sound to the
student who has properly cultivated his sense of cadence.

This case is extremely misleading; it is hard to believe (and feel)
that the characteristic onset of the 16th-triplet figure does not
herald the new phrase; but all the indications of strict, unswerv-
ing analysis (not to be duped by appearances) point to the fact
that this is one of the common cases of disguised cadence, and
not an elision of the cadence.   The *sforzando* marks of Beethoven
confirm this view, and, as in Example 27, we have our four measures to the next cadence, without this " cadence-measure."

The characteristic traits of all these various phases of cadence
formation are : —

(1) That the actual cadence-tone in the melody may be of any time-value, from the full extent of the cadence-measure down to the smallest fraction of that measure. In Ex. 19 it was the former, unbroken; in Ex. 17, No. 1, also, but broken into the six pulses of the measure ; in Ex. 20 it was shortened, by a rest, to one-half its real value ; in Ex. 26 it was reduced to one-quarter of its true value ; in Ex. 25, to one 8th-note ; and in Ex. 24, No. 3, to one 16th-note.

(2) That the cadence-tone in the melody may be shifted forward to almost any point beyond its expected position upon the primary accent. In Ex. 20 (and many other of the given illustrations) it stands in its legitimate place, at the beginning of the measure; in Ex. 21 it stands upon the *second* accent of the measure; in Ex. 22, No. 1, on the second beat in 3–4 measure; in Ex. 22, No. 5, on the third beat of the triple-measure; in Ex. 22, No. 4, on the last eighth note in the measure.

(3) That in almost every case the effect of absolute cessation is softened by marking the rhythm of the cadence-measure ; in no case is the rhythm permitted to pause (not even in Ex. 19, where the accompaniment, not shown, is carried along in unbroken 8th-notes). In some part or other, by some means or other, the cadence-measure is kept alive ; either by continuing the accompaniment, as in Exs. 18 and 20, or by quickly picking up a new rhythm, as in Exs. 27 and 28. Conspicuous exceptions to this rule will be found, it is true, in hymn-tunes and the like; though occasionally even there, as the student may recall, the rhythm, in some cadence-measures, is carried along by one or more of the inner voices; for example, in the hymn-tune " Lead, Kindly Light," of J. B. Dykes. (See also Ex. 29.)

Species of Cadence. — In text-books and musical dictionaries several varieties of the cadence are distinguished, but they are chiefly distinctions without any more than one essential point of difference, namely, difference in force or weight. It is therefore feasible to reduce all these varieties to two, — the heavy cadence and the light cadence. The former is represented by the so-called Perfect cadence, the latter by the many grades of Semicadence.

Perfect Cadence. — There is one method of checking the current of the melodic phrase with such emphasis and determination as to convey the impression of finality; either absolute finality, as we observe it at the very end of a composition, or such relative finality as is necessary for the completion of some independent section of the piece, — conclusive as far as that section is concerned, though not precluding the addition of other sections to this, after the desired degree of repose has been felt. This is known as the perfect cadence, or full stop. It is always made upon the *tonic harmony* of some key as cadence-chord, with the *keynote itself in both outer parts,* and — when desired in its strongest form (without such disguising as we have seen) — upon an *accented beat,* and of somewhat longer duration than its fellow tones. For illustration : —

SCHUBERT.
Perf. cad.

Ex.
29.

At the end of this four-measure phrase there is a perfect cadence, exhibited in its strongest, most conclusive form. It is practically undisguised, though the cadence-chord is reduced to three beats (from the four to which it is entitled) to make room for the preliminary beat of the next phrase (calculated to correspond to the one at the beginning of this phrase).

The cadence-chord is the tonic harmony of C minor; upon the primary accent of the 4th measure; it is considerably longer than any other tone in the phrase; and the keynote *c* is placed both at the top and at the bottom of the harmonic body. See

also Ex. 15 ; the cadence is perfect, because the cadence-chord,
on the accent of the 4th measure, is the tonic harmony of
G major, with the keynote as highest and as lowest tone. It is
abbreviated by rests, which very slightly diminish its weight. Ex.
17, No. 2, closes with a perfect cadence ; it is the tonic harmony
of C major, on an accent, and with the keynote in the two extreme parts. See also Ex. 20.

In the following :

the cadence-chord stands upon the secondary accent (3d beat) of
the final measure. This method of shifting the cadence forward
is generally adopted in large species of measure (6–8, 9–8, and the
like), and has been defined among the devices employed in disguising or *lightening* the cadence. In Ex. 22, No. 5, the cadence-
chord is shifted to the last beat (unaccented) of the final measure ;
this lightens the cadence very materially, but it does not affect
any of its essential properties as perfect cadence. The following
is similar : —

The cadence-chord occupies the unaccented (2d) beat, and is
no longer than any other chord in the phrase. Despite its striking brevity, it is nevertheless a perfect cadence, disguised ; it is
the tonic chord of C major, with the keynote at top and bottom.
See also Ex. 23, No. 1.

The following illustrations come under the head of the disguised cadences seen in Ex. 24 : —

In No. 1 the cadence is perfect, for it is the tonic chord of G major, keynote *g* at top and bottom, and on the primary accent of the fourth measure; but the uninterrupted continuation of the movement of 16ths, in the right hand, shortens the uppermost keynote to a single 16th-note, and would entirely conceal the cadence, were it not for the distinct evidence of repose in the lower part.

In No. 2 the movement in the upper part appears to shatter the cadence; the keynote does not appear on the accent, and its

announcement at the end of the first triplet is very brief.   For all
that, it is an unmistakable perfect cadence ; the chord thus shat-
tered (or " broken," technically speaking) is the tonic harmony of
the key, and the keynote *does* appear as uppermost (and therefore
most prominent) tone, in the same order of percussion as that
given to each of the preceding melody tones.

*   *   *

At the end of an entire piece of music, or of some larger section of the piece, the cadence-chord, on the other hand, is often
lengthened considerably, for the sake of the greater weight and
decision of cadential interruption required at that place. Thus : —

The last two measures are merely the prolongation of the final
cadence-chord.   See also, Mendelssohn, Songs Without Words,
No. 4, last five measures ; No. 8, last eight measures ; and others.

Another peculiarity of the final cadence is, that sometimes the
uppermost tone is the 3d or 5th of the tonic chord, instead of the
keynote, — a significant device to counteract the dead weight of
the cadence-chord, especially when prolonged as just seen.   See
No. 10 of the Songs Without Words, last six measures ; it is the
tonic chord of B minor, but the tone *d* (the 3d) is placed at the
top, instead of *b*.   Also No. 16, last chord ; No. 38, last chord ;
No. 6, last three measures (the 5th of the tonic chord as uppermost tone).   At any other point in the piece this default of the
keynote would, as we shall presently see, almost certainly reduce

the weight of the cadence from "perfect" to "semicadence"; at the very end, however, it cannot mislead, because it does not affect the condition of actual finality.

Semicadence. — Any deviation from the formula of the perfect cadence — either in the choice of some other than the tonic chord, or in the omission of the keynote in either (or both) of the outer parts — weakens the force of the interruption, and transforms the cadence into a lighter, more transient, point of repose, for which the term semicadence (or half-stop) is used. The semicadence indicates plainly enough the end of its phrase, but does not completely sever it from that which follows.

It is these lighter, transient forms of cadence to which a number of different names are given; for the student of analysis (and the composer, also, for that matter) the one general term "semicadence," or half-cadence, is sufficient, and we shall use no other.

If, then, a cadence is final in its effect, it is a perfect one; if not, it is a semicadence. The harmony most commonly chosen as the resting-place of a semicadence is the chord of the *dominant*, — the fifth step of the momentary key, — that being the harmony next in importance to that of the tonic (the one invariably used for the perfect cadence). The following example illustrates the dominant semicadence : —

The cadence-chord is the dominant harmony (root *e*) in the key of A minor; neither of the two upper tones on the first and second beats is the root of the chord; it is quite sufficient that the root appears as lowermost tone, and even this is not necessary. The "point of repose" is shifted to the second beat, in the manner so amply illustrated in the examples of the disguised cadence; the methods we have seen may be applied to *any* kind of cadence.

See also Ex. 18; the key, and therefore the chord, at the semicadence is the same as that of the above example (simply major instead of minor).

Also Ex. 23, No. 4; the semicadence chord is the dominant harmony of E-flat major; it is skillfully disguised. Ex. 25, dominant harmony of A major. Ex. 26, last four measures; the semicadence is made upon the dominant of C minor.

In the following:

the semicadence in the fourth measure is made with the dominant harmony of C major (the tones *g-b-d-f*); it is so disguised as to remove all signs of interruption; but the chord *prevails* throughout the measure, and (as may be seen by reference to the original, op. 68, No. 3) the next measure — the fifth — exactly corresponds to the first; this indicates another "beginning," and proves our "ending."

But though the dominant is thus generally employed at the semicadence, it is by no means the only available chord. It must be remembered that every cadence which does not fulfil the definite conditions of the perfect cadence, is a semicadence. Examine each of the following, and determine why the point of repose is each time a semicadence: — Ex. 1; Ex 9, No. 3; Ex. 14, No. 2, fourth measure; Ex. 14, No. 3, fourth measure; Ex. 19; Ex. 22, Nos. 3 and 4; Ex. 23, No. 2, fourth measure.

The distinction between the two species of cadence becomes most subtle when the *tonic harmony* is chosen for the semicadence, *but with some other part of the chord than the keynote as uppermost (or lowermost) tone.* This might appear to lighten the perfect cadence too immaterially to exercise so radical an influence upon the value (weight) of the interruption. The *keynote*, however, is so decisive and final in its harmonic and melodic effect — everywhere in music — that its absence more or less completely cancels the terminating quality of the cadence-chord; in other words, the force of a tonic cadence depends upon the weight and prominence of the *keynote*.

For example :

The first, second, and third of these cadences is made upon the tonic harmony, on the accent of each successive fourth measure. But they are only *semicadences*, as the melody (uppermost part) rests upon the Third of the chord, *c*, instead of the keynote; this substitution of *c* for *a-flat* is sufficient to frustrate the perfect cadence and diminish it to a transient interruption. The final cadence is perfect, however, because there the uppermost tone *is*

the keynote. See also Ex. 21 ; and Ex. 17, No. 2, fourth measure (semicadence, with *a* instead of *f* as principal tone in upper part, and disguised by the continuation of rhythmic movement to the end of the cadence-measure). In Ex. 17, No. 1, the cadence is made with the tonic harmony of G minor, but with the Third (*b-flat*) at the top.

Locating the Cadences. — Next to the recognition and comparison of the different melodic sections of a composition (in a word, the *melodic delineation* of the whole), the most significant task in music analysis is the locating and classifying of the cadences. They are the angles of the design, so to speak ; and have the same bearing upon the sense of the music as punctuation marks have in rhetoric. Intelligent and effective phrasing, adequate interpretation of the composer's purpose, is impossible without a distinct exposition of the cadences, — if not of the inferior points of interruption between motives, also.

The best general rule for locating cadences is, probably, to look for them in the right place, namely, in the *fourth measure* from the beginning of each phrase. The fairly regular operation of this rule has been verified in Lesson 4. But exceptions have also been seen (in Ex. 17), and many more are certain to be encountered, simply because the principle of Unity (exemplified by the prevalence of the four-measure standard) must interact with the principle of Variety (exemplified in all phrases of irregular extent).

Therefore, the more reliable method, as already stated, is *to define the beginning of the following phrase*, — for each successive beginning involves a foregone cadence, of course. No very definite directions can be given ; experience, observation, careful study and comparison of the given illustrations, will in time surely enable the student to recognize the " signs " of a beginning, — such as the recurrence of some preceding principal member of the melody, or some such change in melodic or rhythmic character as indicates that a new phrase is being announced.

Lesson 5. Analyze, again, Schumann, *Jugend Album* (op. 68), No. 6, locating every cadence and defining its quality, — as perfect cadence or semicadence. Also Nos. 22, 24, 26, 28, 30, 33, 14, 15, 16, 3, — and others. As a curious illustration of the difficulty which may sometimes attend the analysis of phrases and cadences, the student may glance at No. 31 (*Kriegslied*, D major) ; a more baffling example will rarely be found, for the piece abounds in irregular phrase-dimensions, and cadences that are disguised to the verge of unrecognizability ; the only fairly reliable clue the composer has given lies in the formation of the melodic members (the clue intimated in the explanatory text following Ex. 35).

Also Mendelssohn, Songs Without Words, No. 34 (first phrase six measures long) ; No. 40 ; No. 18.

Also Beethoven's pianoforte sonata, op. 22, third movement (*Menuetto*) ; op. 28, second movement (*Andante*).

Again the student is reminded that it is not only permissible, but wise and commendable, to pass by all confusing cases ; without being careless or downright superficial, to observe a certain degree of prudent indifference at confusing points, trusting to that superior intelligence which he shall surely gain through wider experience.

CHAPTER VI. IRREGULAR PHRASES.

Causes. — The possibility of deviating from the fundamental standard of phrase-dimension (four measures) has been repeatedly intimated, and is treated with some detail in the text preceding Example 17, which should be reviewed.   It is now necessary to examine some of the conditions that lead to this result.

The causes of irregular phrase-dimension are two-fold; it may result

(1) from simply inserting an additional cadence, or from omitting one.   Or

(2) it may be the consequence of some specific manipulation of the phrase-melody with a view to its extension or expansion, its development into a broader and more exhaustive exposition of its contents.

The Small and Large Phrases. — If a cadence is inserted before it is properly due, it is almost certain to occur exactly *half-way* along the line toward the expected (regular) cadence, — that is, in the *second* measure.   This is likely to be the case only when the tempo is so slow, or the measures of so large a denomination, that two of them are practically equal to four *ordinary* measures. By way of distinction, such a two-measure phrase is called a Small phrase.   For example : —

There is no reasonable doubt of the semicadence in the second measure, because enough pulses have been heard, up to that point,

60

to represent the sum of an ordinary phrase. If this were written in 6–8 measure (as it might be), it would contain four measures. See, also, Song No. 22 of Mendelssohn, — 9–8 measure, adagio tempo; the phrases are "Small"; note particularly the last two measures. The same is true in No. 17. About Schumann, op. 68, No. 43 (*Sylvesterlied*), there may be some doubt; but the measures, though of common denomination, contain so many tones, in moderate tempo, that the effect of a cadence is fairly complete in the second measure.

If, on the other hand, one of the regular cadences is omitted, — owing to the rapidity of the tempo, or a small denomination of measure, — the phrase will attain just double the ordinary length; that is, *eight* measures. An eight-measure phrase is called a Large phrase. For illustration : —

to represent the sum of an ordinary phrase.

There is not the slightest evidence of repose or interruption in the fourth measure, nor of a new beginning in the fifth, wherefore the cadence is not expected until four more measures have passed by. The inferior points of repose in the upper parts, at the beginning of the 5th, 6th and 7th measures, serve only to establish melodic, or rather rhythmic, variety, and have no cadential force whatever. See Mendelssohn, Song No. 8 ; the first cadence appears to stand in the *eighth* measure; the tempo is rapid and the measures are small; it is obviously a large phrase. The phrase which follows is regular, however ; there *is* a cadence in the twelfth measure, thus proving that Large phrases may appear in company with regular phrases, in the same composition. In other words, the omission of an expected cadence (or the insertion of an additional one) may be an *occasional* occurrence, — not necessarily constant. See, again, No. 22 of the Songs Without Words; the first and second phrases are small; the third phrase, however (reaching from measure 6 to 9 without cadential interruption), is of regular dimensions.

The Principle of Extension. — The other cause of modified phrase-dimension is one of extreme importance, as touching upon the most vital process in musical composition, namely, that of *phrase-development.*

Setting aside all critical discussion with reference to the question, " What is good music? " and simply accepting those types of classic composition universally acknowledged to be the best, as a defensible standard (to say the least), we find that such a page of music exhibits the pursuit of some leading thought (melodic motive or phrase), with precisely the same coherence and consistency, the same evidence of determined aim, as is displayed in the creation of a forcible essay, a masterly poem, an imposing architectural plan, or any other work of art that betrays intelligence and a definite, fixed, purpose. This is no more nor less than might be expected from the dominion of the law of Unity.

The equally inflexible demands of Variety are satisfied by presenting this self-same leading thought in ever new and changing aspects, — *not* by exchanging the thought itself for a new one at each successive angle. This latter faulty process would naturally lead to a conglomeration of impressions, baffling comprehension and jeopardizing real enjoyment.

In a classic page of music we perceive that each successive unit grows, more or less directly, out of those which go before; not so directly, or with such narrow insistence as to produce the impression of sameness and monotony, but with such consistency of design as to impart a unified physiognomy to the whole. Hence,

it will often be found that every melodic figure, during a certain
section (if not the whole) of a composition, may be traced to one
or another of the figures which characterized the first phrase, or
the first two or three phrases, of the piece.   This was emphasized
by our reference, near the end of the first chapter, to the 8th
Song Without Words of Mendelssohn.   If the student, in analyzing
the melody of that composition, will endeavor to penetrate some
of the clever disguises employed by the composer (for the sake
of Variety), he will find the whole piece reducible to a very few
melodic figures, announced at or near the beginning.   See also
No. 45 (C major), No. 36, No. 26.   Also Schumann, op. 68, No.
7, No. 8, No. 18, No. 23.   Also Beethoven, pianoforte sonata, op.
10, No. 2, last movement ; op. 26, last movement.

In musical composition this process is known as thematic development, and it generally extends over the whole, or a greater
part, of the piece.

Its operation on a smaller scale, with more limited reference to one
phrase alone, effects the development of the phrase *by extension.*

The process of extension or expansion, by means of which the
phrase usually assumes a somewhat irregular length, consists
mainly in the varied repetition of the figures or motives that it contains ; and the continuity of the whole, as extension of the *one
phrase*, is maintained by suppressing the cadence — suspending all
cadential interruption — during the lengthening process.   For
example :

These six measures result from a repetition (variated) of the third and fourth measures of the original — regular — four-measure phrase. A cadence is due in the fourth measure, but it is not permitted to assert itself; and if it did, its cadential force would be neutralized by the entirely obvious return to (repetition of) the motive just heard. Further :—

Reproductions of foregoing figure.

There is no cadence in the fourth measure, — the current of the melody obliterates it and hurries on, voicing the last measure again and again until it dies away in the tenth measure, where a cadence ends it. That it should be the *tenth* measure is purely accidental; the number of measures is of little account in the act of extension; here, it was continued until a convenient place was found (with reference to chord and key) for the cadence. Further :—

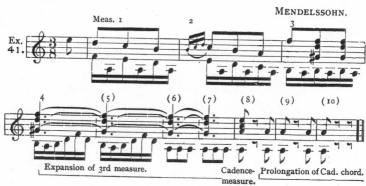

Expansion of 3rd measure.   Cadence-measure.   Prolongation of Cad. chord.

Measures 1, 2, 3 and 8 constitute the original regular four-measure phrase.

The following regular phrase (to be found in the last movement of Beethoven's pianoforte sonata, op. 28) : —

is immediately followed by this lengthy and elaborate extension : —

The portion marked *b* is a complete repetition, with quaint variation, of the original four-measure phrase, marked *a* in Ex. 42 ; *c*
is a repetition of the last figure (just one measure) of the phrase,
with the melodic parts inverted, or exchanged ; *d* and *e* are a
literal repetition of the two preceding measures — (*c*) and *c* ; *f* is
another recurrence of (*c*), with still another inversion of the
melodies ; *g* repeats *e* an octave higher ; and *h* is nothing more
or less than a curious repetition of *g*, in longer tones, and in
reversed direction.   Distinct cadential interruption is carefully
avoided after the original phrase has been announced, that is,
throughout Ex. 43, — which is the significant proof (borne out
by the manifest identity of the *melodic* members) that these
measures form part and parcel of the original phrase, as extension or development of it, and *not* a new phrase.   The
total length is sixteen measures, developed thus out of the original four.

For an exhaustive explanation of phrase-extension, with all the
technical details, the student is referred to my **Homophonic
Forms,** Chapter III.

*   *   *

Another method of extending a phrase consists in prefacing a
measure or two of purely *introductory* material ; it is, therefore,
rather anticipation than prolongation, and is composed most commonly of the figure of the accompaniment, announced briefly
before the actual phrase-melody begins.

This is shown very clearly in the first measure of the 22d Song Without Words ; also in the first measure of No. 7, No. 31, No. 42, No. 40, and others ; the first *two* measures of No. 34, and No. 1 ; the first *three* measures of No. 19, No. 26, and No. 37, — and needs no further illustration. It emphasizes the necessity of vigilance in defining the correct *starting-point* of the first phrase ; for a mistake at the beginning may interfere seriously with the locating of the cadences (according to our fundamental four-measure rule). For instance, in No. 42 the cadences do *not* fall in the 4th 8th, 12th measures— and so on — but in the 5th, 9th, 13th, 17th, from the very beginning of the piece.

When the introductory passage is longer than *three* measures, it probably constitutes a complete phrase by itself, with its own cadence ; in which case, of course, it must not be analyzed as "extension." For example, at the beginning of No. 29; still more apparently at the beginning of No. 28, No. 41, and others.

*   *   *

Inherent Irregularity. — Finally, — there exists another, third, condition, besides those mentioned at the head of this chapter, whereby a phrase may assume an irregular dimension ; not by doubling or dividing its length (as in the large and small phrases) nor by the processes of extension, — but by an arbitrary and apparently incalculable act of *melodic liberty*, — by allowing the melody to choose its own time for the cadential interruption. This comparatively rare occurrence is illustrated in Ex. 17, No. 1 (five-measure phrase), and Ex. 17, No. 2, second phrase (six measures long). It is true that in each of these cases the " extra " measures might be accounted for as "extension by modified repetition," — for instance, in No. 1 the *second* measure might be called a reproduction (or extension) of the first measure. But cases will be encountered where a phrase of three, five, six, or seven measures will admit of no such analysis. In such instances the student is compelled to rely simply upon the evidence of *the cadence*. As was advised in the context of Ex. 17, he must endeavor to define the phrase by recognition of its "beginning" and "ending," as such; or by exercising his judgment of the "cadential impression." See also Ex. 48, second phrase (six measures).

See Schubert, pianoforte sonata No. 1 (A minor, op. 42) *Scherzo*-movement; first 28 measures, divided into 5 phrases — as demonstrated by the melodic formation — of 5, 5, 5, 7 and 6 measures. Also Schubert, *Impromptu*, op. 90, No. 3, measures 42 to 55 (phrases of 5, 5 and 4 measures.)

Lesson 6. Analyze the following examples, locating the cadences and defining their value (as perfect or semicadence); and determining the nature of each irregular phrase (as small, large, or extended phrase):

Beethoven, pianoforte sonata, op. 22, second movement (*Adagio*), first 30 measures.

Beethoven, pianoforte sonata, op. 28, *Scherzo*-movement.

Beethoven, pianoforte sonata, op. 14, No. 3, *Menuetto*.

Mendelssohn, Songs Without Words: No. 4, first 5 measures.

No. 46, last 9½ measures.

No. 42, last 15 measures.

No. 45, last 11 measures.

No. 12, last 12 measures.

No. 14, last 11 measures.

No. 36, last 22 measures.

No. 37, last 11 measures.

Beethoven, pianoforte sonata, op. 27, No. 2, last movement; measures 7 to 23 from the second double-bar.

Beethoven, pianoforte sonata, op. 28, first movement; from the double-bar (near the middle of the movement) measures 21 to 94 (⌒); in this extraordinary specimen of phrase-development, the original four-measure phrase yields seventy-four successive measures, with very few cadences to divide it even into sections. — Same sonata, last movement, last eighteen measures.

CHAPTER VII. THE PERIOD–FORM.

Phrase-addition. — The phrase is the structural basis of all musical composition. By this is meant, not necessarily the single phrase, but the phrase in its collective sense.

The phrase is, after all, only a unit ; and the requirements of Variety cannot be wholly satisfied by the mere development and extension of a single phrase, except it be for a certain limited section of the piece, or for a brief composition in small form (like Schumann, op. 68, No. 8).

The act of *addition* does therefore enter into the processes of music-writing, as well as *extension.* Phrase may be added to phrase, in order to increase the primary material, and to provide for greater breadth of basis, and a richer fund of resources. The condition to be respected is, that such aggregation shall not become the ruling trait, and, by its excess, supplant the main purpose, — that of *development.* That is, it must be held rigidly within the domain of Unity. The student of the classic page will therefore expect to find a more or less marked family resemblance, so to speak, prevailing throughout the various phrases that may be associated upon that page.

Each additional phrase should be, and as a rule will be, sufficiently " new " in some respect or other to impart renewed energy to the movement ; but — so long as it is to impress the hearer as being the same movement — there will still remain such points of contact with the foregoing phrase or phrases as to demonstrate its derivation from them, its having " grown out " of them.

This process of addition (not to be confounded with the methods of extending a single phrase, illustrated in the preceding chapter) is exhibited first, and most naturally, in the so-called Period-form.

The Period. — The Period-form is obtained by the addition of a second phrase to the first. It is therefore, in a sense, a double phrase; that is, it consists of two connected phrases, covering *eight ordinary measures,* or just double the number commonly assigned to the single phrase.

Each one of these phrases must, of course, have its individual cadence, or point of repose; the first — called the *Antecedent phrase* — has its cadence in the fourth measure, and the second — called the *Consequent phrase* — in the eighth measure. The effect of the Period-form is that of a longer sentence interrupted exactly in the middle, — not unlike a bridge of two spans, resting on a central pier. But, precisely as the central pier is only an intermediate point of support, and not terra firma, so the ending of the Antecedent phrase is never anything more weighty than a semicadence, while the definite, conclusive, perfect cadence appears at the end of the Consequent phrase, — or of the entire period-form.

The reason for this distinction of cadence is obvious. A period is not two separate phrases, but two related and coherent phrases which mutually balance each other. The Consequent phrase is not merely an "addition" to the first, but is its complement and "fulfilment." The two phrases represent the musical analogy of what, in rhetoric, would be called thesis and antithesis, or, simply, question and answer. In a well-constructed period the Antecedent phrase is, therefore, always more or less *interrogative,* and the Consequent phrase *responsive,* in character.

For illustration (Mendelssohn, No. 28) : —

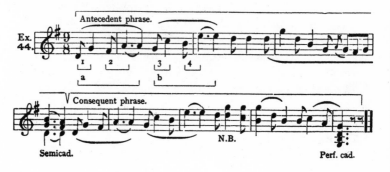

The co-operation, or interaction, of the principles of Unity and Variety, is nowhere more strikingly shown than in the formulation of the musical period. Either element has the right to predominate, to a reasonable degree, though never to the exclusion or injury of the other. In the above example, the principle of Unity predominates to a somewhat unusual extent : — not only the figures (marked 1–2–3–4), and the motives (*a–b*), are uniform, in the Antecedent phrase itself, but the melody of the Consequent phrase corresponds very closely throughout to that of the Antecedent, only excepting a trifling change in the course (marked *N. B.*), and the last few tones, which are necessarily so altered as to transform the semicadence into a perfect cadence. It is this significant change, *at the cadence*, which prevents the second phrase from being merely a "repetition" of the first one, — which makes it a "Consequent," a response to the one that precedes.

Further (Mendelssohn, No. 23) : —

In this example also, the Consequent phrase is a complete affirmation of its Antecedent, agreeing in its melodic form with the latter until the cadence is nearly due, when an extra measure is inserted (as extension), and the usual digression into the necessary perfect cadence is made. The condition of Unity predominates, but a noticeable infusion of Variety takes place.

Further (Mozart, pianoforte sonata) : —

Here, again, the condition of Unity prevails, but with a still greater infusion of Variety ; the melody of the Consequent phrase *resembles* that of the Antecedent in every detail; the rhythm is identical, and it is evident that the second phrase is designed to balance the first, figure for figure, the principal change being that some of the figures are simply turned upside down (compare the places marked *N. B.*).   The semicadence rests upon a dominant chord (fifth-step) of D major ; the perfect cadence upon the same chord, it is true, but as *tonic* harmony of A major, with keynote in the extreme parts.   Being a keynote, though not in the original key, it is valid as perfect cadence.

Further (Beethoven, pianoforte sonata, op. 13) : —

In this example, the condition of Variety predominates decidedly. The Consequent melody differs totally from the Antecedent, even in rhythm, and the necessary portion of Unity is exhibited only in equality of length, *uniformity of accompaniment*, and similarity of character (tonality, and general harmonic and rhythmic effect). Observe the diversity of melodic extent; in the two phrases, in consequence of the preliminary tone borrowed from the semicadence for the Consequent phrase. Greater variety than here will rarely be found between two successive phrases that are intended to form the halves of one coherent period.

For more minute technical details see the **Homophonic Forms,** Chapter V.

Lesson 7. Analyze the following examples. Locate the cadences; compare the phrases and define the degrees of Unity and of Variety exhibited in the melody, or elsewhere; and mark such irregularities of forms (or extensions) as may be found: —

Mendelssohn, Songs Without Words, No. 35, measures 5 ½–13. (By 5 ½ is meant the *middle* of the fifth measure, instead of its beginning.)

No. 45, first 8 measures.

No. 29, measures 4 ½–12.

No. 14, " 1–8.

No. 34, " 1–10.

No. 18, " 1–9; 10–17.

No. 9, " 3 ½–7.

No. 27, " 5–12.

Schumann, op. 68, No. 3, measures 1–8; 9–16.

No. 5, measures 1–8; 9–16. (Do not overlook the preliminary tones which precede the first measure.)

The first eight measures of Nos. 6, 7, 8, 9, 11, 12, 15, 22, 23, 24, 26, 30, 32, 39.   Also Nos. 13 and 28, first *ten* measures.

Beethoven, pianoforte sonatas : op. 2, No. 1, *Adagio*, measures 1–8.   Same sonata, third movement, "Trio," measures 1–10.

Op. 2, No. 2, *Largo*, measures 1–8 ; also *Scherzo*, measures 1–8 ; also *Rondo*, measures 1–8.

Op. 2, No. 3, measures 1–13 ; also *Scherzo*, measures 1–16 ; also last movement, measures 1–8.

Op. 10, No. 1, *Finale*, measures 1–8 ; and measures 16½–28.

Op. 10, No. 3, measures 1–10 ; also *Largo*, measures 1–9 ; 9½–17 ; also *Menuetto*, measures 1–16 ; also *Rondo*, measures 1–9.

Op. 14, No. 2, measures 1–8 ; also *Andante*, measures 1–8 ; also *Scherzo*, measures 1–8.

After analyzing these examples, the student may venture to define the periods in other compositions, classic or popular, especially such as he may chance to be learning.

CHAPTER VIII. — ENLARGEMENT OF THE PERIOD-FORM.

THE processes of extension and development are applied to the period in the same general manner as to the phrase. The results, however, are broader; partly because every operation is performed on a correspondingly larger scale, and partly because the resources of technical manipulation increase, naturally, with the growth of the thematic material.

Among the various methods adopted, there are three, each significant in its own peculiar way, that provide sufficiently exhaustive directions for the student of structural analysis.

Enlargement by Repetition. — The first and simplest method is to increase the length of the period-form by the process of *repetition;* repetition of the entire sentence, or of any one — or several — of its component members, in a manner very similar to that already seen in connection with the single phrase (Chap. VI, Ex. 39, etc.), and under the same conditions of Unity and Variety; that is, the repetitions may be nearly or quite literal, or they may have been subjected to such alterations and variations as the skill and fancy of the composer suggested.

An example of complete repetition (that is, the repetition of the entire period), with simple but effective changes, may be found in Beethoven, pianoforte sonata, op. 13, *Adagio*, measures 1 to 16. Examine it carefully, and observe, among other details, the treatment of the perfect cadence (in the 8th measure). See also, Song Without Words, No. 27, measures 5 to 20.

The repetition of one of the two phrases is exhibited in the following (Mozart, sonata No. 14) : —

The Antecedent is a regular four-measure phrase, with semi-cadence (made on the tonic chord, but with *3d* as uppermost tone); the Consequent is a six-measure phrase, with perfect cadence, and is repeated, with partial change of register. The whole is a "period with repeated Consequent."

A somewhat elaborate example of extension by detail-repetition is seen in the following (Chopin, Mazurka No. 20, op. 30, No. 3, — see the original):

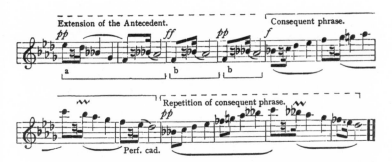

These sixteen measures are the product out of eight measures, by extension; that is, they are reducible to a simple period-form (as may be verified by omitting the passages indicated under dotted lines), and they represent in reality nothing more than its manipulation and development. The original 8-measure period makes a complete musical sentence, and was so devised in the mind of the composer, *without the extensions.* The method of manipulation is ingenious; observe the variety obtained by the striking dynamic changes from *ff* to *pp*; and, hand in hand with these, the changes from major to minor, and back (as shown by the inflection of *b*-flat to *b*-double-flat). These are first applied to members only, of the Antecedent, as indicated by the brackets *a* and *b*, and then to the entire Consequent phrase. Observe, also, that in the repeated form of the latter, the rhythm is modified to a smoother form, during two measures. The result here achieved is constant Unity and constant Variety from almost every point of view, admirably counterbalanced.

The Phrase-group. — A second method consists in enlarging the period-form to three phrases, by the same process of addition which, as explained in the preceding chapter, transforms the single phrase into the double-phrase or period. In order to preserve the continuity of the three phrases, it is evident that the second phrase must *also* close with a semicadence, — the perfect cadence being deferred until the last phrase is concluded.

This form, be it well understood, does not include any of the
triple-phrase designs which may result from merely *repeating* one
or the other of the two phrases that make a period, as is shown in
Ex. 48. *All such phrase-clusters as are reducible to two phrases,*
because nothing more than simple repetition has been employed
in their multiplication, should always be classed among ordinary
periods ; for two successive phrases, if connected (that is, unless
they are purposely broken asunder by a definite perfect cadence
at the end of the first phrase) always represent the analogy of
Question and Answer.

The enlarged form we are at present considering consists of
three *different* phrases, as a general rule ; probably very closely
related, or even distinctly resembling one another ; but too independent, nevertheless, to constitute actual repetition, and therefore
to admit of reduction to two phrases. For this very reason it
cannot justly be called " period " at all, but takes the name of
" phrase-group." An illustration by diagram will make the distinction clear : —

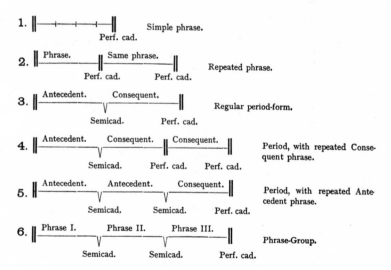

Observe that the classification depends upon the number of phrases, — upon the *melodic* identity of the phrases, — and upon the *quality of the cadences.*

No. 1 is illustrated in Ex. 15 ; No. 2, in Ex. 42 and the first four measures of Ex. 43 (cadence not perfect, it is true, but same phrase-melody and *same cadence*) ; No. 3 is seen in Ex. 44 (phrase-melody similar, but cadences different) — also in Ex. 47 ; No. 4 is seen in Ex. 48 ; No. 5 is rare, but an example will be discovered in Lesson 8 ; No. 6 is illustrated in the following (Grieg, op. 38, No. 2) : —

Comparing this sentence with Ex. 48, we discover the following significant difference : There, no more than two phrases were present ; the whole sentence was *reducible* to two phrases. Here (Ex. 50), however, no such reduction is possible ; three sufficiently similar — and sufficiently different — phrases are coherently connected, without evidence of mere repetition ; it is the result of Addition, and the form is a *phrase-group.* The first cadence is, strictly speaking, a *perfect* one ; but of that somewhat doubtful rhythmic character, which, in conjunction with other indications, may diminish its conclusive effect, and prevent the decided separation which usually attends the perfect cadence. This is apt to be the case with a perfect cadence *so near the beginning* (like this one) that the impression of " conclusion " is easily overcome. In a word, there is no doubt of the unbroken connection of these three phrases, despite the unusual weight of the first cadence. See also the first cadence in Ex. 51.

By simply continuing the process of addition (and avoiding a decisive perfect cadence) the phrase-group may be extended to more than three phrases, though this is not common.

The Double-period. — A third method consists in expanding the period into a double-period (precisely as the phrase was lengthened into a double-phrase, cr period), *by avoiding a perfect cadence at the end of the second phrase*, and adding another pair of phrases to balance the first pair. It thus embraces four *coherent* phrases, with a total length of sixteen measures (when regular and unextended).

An important feature of the double-period is that the second period usually resembles the first one very closely, at least in its first members. That is, the second phrase contrasts with the first ; *the third corroborates the first ;* and the fourth either resembles the second, or contrasts with all three preceding phrases. This is not always — though nearly always — the case.

The double-period in music finds its poetic analogy in almost any stanza of four fairly long lines, that being a design in which we expect unity of meaning throughout, the progressive evolution of one continuous thought, uniformity of metric structure (mostly in *alternate* lines), the corroboration of rhyme, and, at the same time, some degree and kind of contrast, — as in the following stanza of Tennyson's :

> Phrase 1.   "The splendor falls on castle walls,
> Phrase 2.   And snowy summits old in story ;
> Phrase 3.   The long light shakes across the lakes,
> Phrase 4.   And the wild cataract leaps in glory."

The analogy is not complete; one is not likely to find, anywhere, absolute parallelism between music and poetry; but it is near enough to elucidate the musical purpose and character of the double-period. And it accounts for the very general choice of this form for the hymn-tune.

The following illustrates the double-period, in its most regular and convincing form (Beethoven, pianoforte sonata, op. 49, No. 1):—

Each phrase is four measures long, as usual; the first one ends (as in Ex. 50) with one of those early, transient perfect cadences that do not break the continuity of the sentence; the second phrase ends with a semicadence, — therefore the sentence remains unbroken; phrase three is *exactly* like the first, and is therefore an Antecedent, as before; phrase four bears close resemblance to the second one, but differs at the end, on account of the perfect cadence.   The evidences of Unity and Variety are easily detected. The main points are, that the second pair of phrases balances the first pair, and that the two periods are connected (not *separate* periods).   See also Ex. 53, first 16 measures.

Lesson 8. — Analyze the following examples.   They are not classified ; therefore the student must himself determine to which of the above three species of enlargement each belongs :

Mendelssohn, Songs Without Words, No. 29, measures 1–21, (first 4 measures an introductory phrase).

No. 37, first 17 measures.

No. 30, first 15 measures (last phrase irregular).

No. 16, measures 4–9 (small phrases).

No. 33, first 12 measures.

No. 27, first 20 measures (introductory phrase).

No. 3, first 29 measures, to double-bar (introductory phrase).

No. 36, first 27 measures (the similarity between phrase one and phrase three proves the double-period form ; the extra phrases are extension by "addition," as in the group form).

No. 6, measures 8–17.

Mozart, pianoforte sonata, No. 13 (Peters edition), first 16 measures.

Sonata No. 2, first 16 measures (last four measures are extension).

Sonata No. 3, last movement, first 16 measures.

Sonata No. 10, second movement, first 16 measures.

Beethoven, pianoforte sonatas ; op. 49, No. 2, first 12 measures.

Op. 10, No. 3, first 16 measures.

Op. 10, No. 2, first 12 measures.

Op. 26, first 16 measures.

Op. 31, No. 2, last movement, first 31 measures (extension by repetition).

Schumann, op. 68, Nos. 16, 20, 33, first 16 measures of each ; No. 13, first 10 measures ; No. 15, first 16 measures.

CHAPTER IX. THE TWO-PART SONG-FORM.

The Song-form or Part-form. — Almost every musical composition of average (brief) dimensions, if designed with the serious purpose of imparting a clear formal impression, will admit of division into either two or three fairly distinct sections, or Parts, of approximately equal length. The distinctness with which the points of separation are marked, and the degree of independence of each of these two or three larger sections, are determined almost entirely by the length of the whole. And whether there be two or three such divisions depends to some extent also upon the length of the piece, though chiefly upon the specific structural idea to be embodied.

A composition that contains two such sections is called a Two-Part (or bipartite, or binary) form ; and one that contains three, a Three-part (tripartite, or ternary) form.

Such rare exceptions to these structural arrangements as may be encountered in musical literature, are limited to sentences that, on one hand, are so brief as to require no radical division ; and, on the other, to compositions of very elaborate dimensions, extending beyond this structural distinction ; and, furthermore, to fantastic pieces in which the intentional absence of classified formal disposition is characteristic and essential.

The terms employed to denote this species (" Song-form " or " Part-form ") do not signify that the music is necessarily to be a vocal composition of that variety known as the " Song " ; or that it is to consist of several voices (for which the appellation " parts " is commonly used). They indicate simply a certain *grade*, — not a specific variety, — of form ; an intermediate grade between the smallest class (like brief hymn-tunes, for example), and the largest class (like complete sonata-movements). An excellent type of this grade of Form is found in the Songs Without Words of Mendelssohn, the Marzurkas of Chopin, and works of similar extent.

The word Part (written always with a capital in these lessons) denotes, then, one of these larger sections. The design of the Part-forms was so characteristic of the early German *lied*, and is so common in the *song* of all eras, that the term " Song-form " seems a peculiarly appropriate designation, irrespective of the vocal or instrumental character of the composition.

The student will perceive that it is the smallest class of forms — the Phrase-forms, — embracing the phrase, period and double-period, to which the preceding chapters have been devoted. These are the designs which, as a general rule, *contain only one decisive perfect cadence*, and that at the end ; and which, therefore, though interrupted by semicadences, *are continuous and coherent*, because the semicadence merely interrupts, and does not sever, the continuity of the sentence. (This grade of forms might be called One-Part forms).

The Parts. — If we inquire into the means employed, in the larger Part-forms, to effect the division of the whole into its broader Parts, we find that the prime factors, here again, are Cadence and Melody. The strongest sign of the consummation of a Part is a *decisive perfect cadence*, resting, as usual, upon the tonic harmony of the chosen key ; a cadence sufficiently emphatic to interrupt the closer cohesion of the phrases which precede, and bring them, as completed Part, to a conclusion. Such a cadence, marking the end of the First Part, may be verified in Mendelssohn's Songs Without Words, No. 23, measure 15 ; No. 3, measure 29 (at the double-bar, — a sign which frequently appears at the termination of Part One) ; No. 20, measure 21 ; No. 27, measure 12 ; No. 34, measure 10.

Another indication of the Part-form is a palpable change in melodic character in passing from one Part into the next ; suffi-cient to denote a more striking " new beginning " than marks the announcement of a new *phrase* only. The change, however, is as a rule *not very marked;* it is sometimes, in fact, so slight as to be no more than simply palpable, though scarcely definable on the page. For these divisions are, after all, the several "Parts" of one and the same song-form, and, therefore, any such radical change in melodic or rhythmic character, or in general style, as would make each Part appear to be a *wholly independent* musical idea (subject or theme), would be manifestly inconsistent.

Generally, both these factors (cadence and melody) unite to define the end of one Part and the beginning of the next. Should either one be feeble, or absent, the other factor will be all the more pronounced. Thus, the cadence of Part One may be less decisive, if the change in melodic character at the beginning of Part Two is well marked; this is seen in No. 33, measure 12. The reverse — a strong cadence and but little melodic change, — in No. 13, measure 20.

The First Part. — Part One may be designed as period, double-period, or phrase-group; sometimes, though very rarely, as single phrase, repeated. It ends, usually, with a strong perfect cadence on the tonic chord of the original key, or of some related key (that is, one whose *signature* closely resembles that of the original key). An introductory phrase, or independent prelude, may precede it.

The Second Part. — Part Two, as intimated, is likely to begin with a more or less palpable change of melodic character, — by no means is this always the case. It may be designed, also, as period, double-period, or phrase-group, and is somewhat likely to be a little longer (more extended) than Part One. A concluding section (called codetta if small, coda if more elaborate) often follows, after a decided perfect cadence in the original key has definitely concluded the Part.

The following is one of the simplest examples of the Two-Part Song-form (a German *lied* by Silcher) : —

PART I. Period-form.

PART II. Period-form.

The whole embraces four phrases, and might, for that reason, be mistaken for a double-period. But the *strong perfect cadence* at the end of the first period (reinforced by the repetition), and the contrasting melodic formation of the second period, so separate and distinguish the two periods as to make them independent "Parts" of the whole. It is not one "double-period," but *two fairly distinct periods.* The first cadence (in measure 4) has again, strictly speaking, the elements of a perfect cadence, but, like others we have seen (Exs. 50, 51), too near the beginning to possess any plausible concluding power.

A somewhat similar specimen may be found in the theme of Mendelssohn's Variations in D minor, op. 54, which see. Each Part is a regular period-form, with correct semicadence and perfect cadence. The problem of "agreement and independence" in the relation of Part II to Part I is admirably solved ; it is a masterly model of well-matched Unity and Variety, throughout.

For a longer and more elaborate example, see No. 6 of the Songs Without Words, in which, by the way, the principle of en- largement by the addition of an independent prefix (introduction) and affix (coda) is also illustrated : —

First number the forty-six measures with pencil.

The first cadence occurs in measure 7, and marks the end of the prelude. Part I begins in measure 8. In measure 11 there is a semicadence, at end of Antecedent phrase ; in measure 17, a strong perfect cadence, which, in connection with the subsequent change of melodic form, distinctly defines the end of Part I (period-form, extended). Part II therefore begins in measure 18. In measures 21, 25, 29, cadences occur, but none conclusive enough to close the Part. This conclusion takes place, however, in measure 34. Part II proves to be a double-period. A coda begins in measure 35 ; its first members resemble the first phrase of Part I. In measure 40 another section of the coda begins, borrowed from the prelude. For exhaustive technical details of the Two-Part Song-form, see the **Homophonic Forms,** Chapters 9 and 10.

Lesson 9. — Analyze the following examples of the Two-Part Song-form. Define the form of each Part, marking and classify- ing all cadences ; and indicate introductions and codas (or codet- tas), if present. *The first step in the analysis of these forms is to divide the whole composition into its Parts, by defining the end of Part One.* The next step is to define the beginning of Part One, and end of Part Two, by separating the introduction and coda (if present) from the body of the form.

Beethoven, pianoforte sonatas : op. 57, *Andante*, Theme.

Op. 109, *Andante*, Theme.

Op. 111, last movement, Theme of Variations.

Op. 79, *Andante*, first 8 measures (unusually small) ; same so- nata, last movement, first 16 measures.

Op. 54, first 24 measures (each Part repeated).

Op. 31, No. 3, *Menuetto* (without Trio).

Op. 26, " Trio " of *Scherzo ;* also last movement, first 28 measures (second Part repeated).

Op. 27, No. 2, " Trio " of *Allegretto.*

Mozart, pianoforte sonatas : No. 2 (Peters edition), *Andante,* measures 1–20 ; and measures 21–40.

Schumann, op. 68, No. 7 ; No. 4 ; No. 35 ; No. 42 ; No. 23 (repeated ; last 16 ½ measures, coda).

CHAPTER X. — THE THREE-PART SONG-FORM.

Distinction between Bipartite and Tripartite Forms. — We learned, in the preceding chapter, that the Two-Part Song-form is a composition of rather brief extent, with so decisive a perfect cadence in its course as to divide it, in a marked manner, into two separate and fairly individual sections or "Parts."

Between this and the next higher form, — that with *three* such Parts, — there is a distinction far more essential and characteristic than that of mere extent; a distinction that does not rest simply upon the number of Parts which they respectively contain. Each of the two classes of formal design, the Two-Part and the Three-Part, embodies a peculiar structural idea; and it is the evidence of these respective ideas, — the true content of the musical form, — which determines the species. The "number" of sections is, in this connection, nothing more than the external index of the inherent idea.

The Two-Part forms embody the idea of *progressive growth*. To the first Part, a second Part (of similar or related melodic contents) is added, in coherent and logical succession. It should not be, and in good clear form it is not, a purely numerical enlargement, for the association of the second Part with a foregoing one answers the purposes of confirmation and of balance, and is supposed to be so effectuated as to institute and maintain unity of style, and some degree of progressive development. But the second Part, in this bipartite design, does little or nothing more, after all, than thus to project the musical thought on outward in a straight line (or along parallel lines) to a conclusion more or less distant from the starting-point, — from the melodic members which constitute the actual germ, or the "text" of the entire musical discourse. A very desirable, not to say vital, condition is therefore lacking, in the Two-Part forms ; namely, the corroboration of this melodic germ by an emphatic return to the beginning and an un-mistakable re-announcement of the first (leading) phrase or phrases of the composition.

Nothing could be more natural than such corroboration. Any line of conduct, if pursued without deviation, simply carries its object farther and farther away from its origin. If, as in the cir-cle, this line is led back to the starting-point, it describes the most satisfying and perfect figure ; it perfects, by enclosing space. Whereas, if it goes straight onward, it ultimately loses itself, or loses, at least, its connection with its beginning and source.

Nowhere is this principle of *Return* more significant and im-perative than in music, which, because of its intangibility, has need of every means that may serve to define and illuminate its design ; and hence the superior frequency and perfection of the Three-Part form, *which, in its Third Part, provides for and executes this Re-turn to the beginning.* Its superiority and greater adaptability is fully confirmed in the practice of composition ; the number of Three-Part forms exceeds the Two-Part, in musical literature, to an almost surprising degree ; and it may therefore be regarded as the design peculiarly adapted to the purposes of ordinary music writing within average limits.

The three successive divisions of the Three-Part Song-form may then be characterized as follows : —

Part I. — The statement of the principal idea ; the presenta-tion of the melodic and rhythmic contents of the leading thought, out of which the whole composition is to be developed. It is gen-erally a period-form, at least, closing with a firm perfect cadence in the principal key, or one of its related keys.

Part II. — The departure (more or less emphatic) from this lead-ing melodic statement. It is, for a time, probably an evident con-tinuation and development of the melodic theme embodied in the First Part ; but it does not end there; it exhibits a retrospective bent, and — when thoroughly legitimate — its last few measures prepare for, and lead into, the melodic member with which the piece began. Its form is optional; but, as a rule, decisive cadence-impressions are avoided, unless it be the composer's intention to *close* it with a perfect cadence (upon any *other* than the principal tonic), and accomplish the "return to the beginning" by means of a separate returning passage, called the Re-transition.

Part III. — The recurrence and corroboration of the original statement; *the reproduction of Part I,* and therewith the fulfilment of the important principle of return and confirmation. The reproduction is sometimes exact and complete; sometimes slight changes, or even striking variations, possibly certain radical alterations, occur; sometimes it is only a partial recurrence, the first few measures being sufficient to prove the "Return"; sometimes, on the other hand, considerable material (more or less related) is added, so that Part III is longer than the First Part.

From this it appears that much latitude is given to the composer, in his formulation of the Third Part. All that the Part has to prove, is its identity as confirmation of the leading motive, and this it may do in many ways, and with great freedom of detail, without obscuring the main purpose. It is precisely this richness of opportunity, this freedom of detail, which enhances the beauty and value of the tripartite forms.

The following is a very regular example of the **Three-Part Song**-form (Schumann, op. 68, No. 20) : —

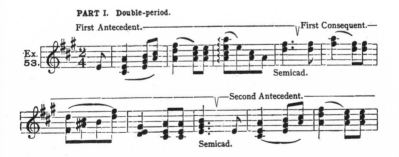

PART II Phrase, repeated.

PART III. Double-period; like Part I.

This version is as complete as it can conveniently be made upon one single staff (chosen in order to economize space); but the student will find the formal design somewhat more plastically defined in the original, complete form, and he is therefore expected to refer to the latter.   Part I is an unusually regular double-period, with three semicadences and a strong perfect cadence, on the original tonic, to mark its conclusion; the double-bar is an additional confirmation of the end of the Part.   The second Part runs in the key of E major (the dominant of the original key) throughout ; its form is only a phrase, but repeated, — as is proven by the almost literal agreement of the second phrase with the preceding one, *cadence and all.* Part III agrees literally with Part I in its melodic formation, but differs a little in the treatment of the lower (accompanying) voices.

In the theme of Mendelssohn's pianoforte Variations in E-flat major (op. 82), which see, the design is as follows : — Part I is a period of eight measures. Part II is also an 8-measure period, ending upon the tonic chord of B-flat major (the dominant key), as first eighth-note of the 16th measure ; the following eighth-note, b-natural, represents what we have called the Retransition (in its smallest conceivable form), as it fulfils no other purpose than that of leading back into the first tone of the First Part. Part III is *only a phrase*, and therefore shorter than Part I ; but it corroborates the *beginning*, and, in fact, the entire contents of the First Part.

The plan of Mendelssohn's 28th Song Without Words is as follows : — First number the 38 measures, *carefully*. The first four measures are an introductory phrase, or prelude ; Part I begins in the second half of measure 4 (after the double-bar) and extends, as regular 8-measure period, to measure 12. Part II follows, during the same measure ; its form is a period, extending to measure 20, and closing with a very distinctly marked semicadence on the dominant chord (chord of D). Part III is 14 measures long, containing therefore six more measures than the First Part ; its first phrase is almost exactly like the first phrase of Part I ; its second phrase (measures 25–28) differs from any portion of Part I, but closely resembles the melodic formation of Part II ; its third phrase is based upon the preceding one (*not* as repetition, however), and is expanded to the 34th measure. The form of Part III is phrase-group. The last four measures are codetta, or postlude, and corroborate the prelude.

For exhaustive technical details of the Three-Part Song-form, see the **Homophonic Forms,** Chapters 11, 12, 13, 14 and 15.

Lesson 10. — Analyze the following examples of the Three-Part Song-form. The first step, here again, is to fix *the end of the First Part ;* the next, to mark the beginning of the Third Part, by determining where the *return to the beginning* is made. These points established, it remains to fix the beginning of Part I, by deciding whether there is an introductory sentence or not ; then the end of Part II, by deciding whether it leads directly into Part III, or comes to a conclusion somewhat earlier, to make room for a Retransition ; then the end of Part III, by deciding whether a codetta or coda has been added. The extremities of the three Parts being thus determined, there will be no difficulty in defining the *form* of each. Very particular attention must be devoted to *the comparison of Part III with Part I*, in order to discover, and accurately define, the difference between them, — in form, in extent, in melodic formation, or in technical treatment.

Mendelssohn, Songs Without Words : No. 22, No. 35, No. 32, No. 45, No. 42, No. 31, No. 27, No. 46, No. 25, No. 20, No. 26 (Re-transition, middle of measure 25 to measure 29) ; No. 36 (beginning of Part III, measure 60, somewhat disguised) ; No. 47, No. 12, No. 15, No. 3, No. 43, No. 40, No. 37, No. 2, No. 33, No. 30, No. 1.

Schumann, op. 68 ; No. 3 ; No. 12, first 24 measures ; No. 14, No. 16, No. 17, No. 21 (Part I closes with a semicadence, but made in such a manner that it answers its purpose without the least uncertainty) ; No. 24, No. 25, No. 26, No. 28 ; No. 29, last 48 measures (including coda) ; No. 33 (long coda) ; No. 34 ; No. 37, first 32 measures ; No. 38 ; No. 40, first movement (2–4 measure) ; No. 41.

Beethoven, pianoforte sonatas : op. 2, No. 1, third movement, — both the *Menuetto* and the *Trio.* Op. 2, No. 2, third movement, — both *Scherzo* and *Trio.* Same sonata, last movement; first 16 measures (Parts II and III consist of a single phrase each ; therefore the whole is diminutive in extent ; but it is unquestiona bly Three-Part Song-form, because of the completeness of Part I, and the unmistakable *return to the beginning*).

Op. 7, *Largo*, first 24 measures. Same sonata, third movement; also the *Minore*. Same sonata, last movement, first 16 measures.

Op. 10, No. 2, second movement, first 38 measures.

Op. 10, No. 3, *Menuetto*.

Op. 14, No. 1, third movement; also the *Maggiore*.

Op. 14, No. 2, second movement, first 20 measures.

Op. 22, *Menuetto;* also the *Minore*.

Op. 26, first 34 measures; same sonata, *Scherzo;* same sonata, *Funeral march* (also the *Trio;* what is its form ?).

Mozart, pianoforte sonatas : No. 15 (Peters Edition), *Andante*, first 32 measures.

No. 1, last movement, first 50 measures.

No. 12, first 18 measures. Same sonata, *Trio* of the second movement (Part III returns to the beginning very briefly, and is otherwise different from the First Part almost throughout).

No. 13, *Adagio*, first 16 measures.

Chopin, *Mazurkas* (Peters edition), No. 11, No. 22, No. 24, No. 40, No. 49.

In the following examples, the student is to determine whether the form is Two-Part or Three-Part : —

Mendelssohn, op. 72 (six pianoforte pieces), No. 1 ; No. 2 ; No. 3, No. 4, No. 6. — Etudes, op. 104, No. 1, No. 3.

A curious example may be found in Schumann, op. 68, No. 32 ; the form is actually Two-Part, but with a very brief reminiscence of the beginning (scarcely to be called a Return) in the *last two measures*, — which are, strictly speaking, no more than a codetta. The Second Part is repeated.

In Schumann's op. 68, Nos. 8, 9, and 11 (first 24 measures), the *second* Part is unusually independent in character ; completely detached from Part III, and exhibiting no symptoms of leading into the latter, as second Parts have commonly been observed to do.

CHAPTER XI. ENLARGEMENT OF THE THREE–PART SONG–FORM.

Repetition of the Parts. — The enlargement of the Three-Part Song-form is effected, in the majority of cases, by simply repeating the Parts. The composer, in extending the dimensions of his original design, resorts as usual to the most legitimate and natural means at his disposal — that of *repetition*. By so doing, he reinforces the principle of Unity, and, instead of obscuring, places the contents of his design in a stronger and more convincing light. It is true that the act of mere repetition involves the risk of monotony; but against this the composer has an efficient safeguard, — that of *variation*. He may modify and elaborate the repetition in any manner and to any extent that seems desirable or necessary, the only limitations being that the identity of the original Part must be preserved beyond all danger of misapprehension, and (as a rule) that the cadences shall not be altered.

The act of repetition is applied to the First Part alone, and to the *Second and Third Parts together;* very rarely to the Second Part alone, or to the Third Part alone.

Exact Repetitions. — When Part I, — or Parts II and III together, — are to be repeated without any changes, it is customary to employ the familiar repetition-marks (double-bar and dots); with " first and second ending," if, for any reason, some modification of the cadence-measure is required. This is illustrated in the 7th Song Without Words; Part I is repeated alone, and Parts II and III together; both repetitions are indicated by the customary signs, and each has a double ending. See also, Schumann, op. 68, No. 1; Part I is repeated exactly, with repetition-marks); Parts II and III are also repeated literally (all but the very last tone in the lower part), but written out, — apparently without necessity. Also No. 2 ; the literal repetition of Part I is written out ; Parts II and III have the repetition-marks.

Modified Repetitions. — The quality and extent of the changes that may be made, in order to enrich the composition without altering its structural design, depend, as has been intimated, upon the judgment and fancy of the composer. The student will find no part of his analytical efforts more profitable and instructive than the careful comparison of these modified repetitions with the original Parts ; nothing can be more fascinating and inspiring to the earnest musical inquirer, than thus to trace the operation of the composer's mind and imagination ; to witness his employment of the technical resources in re-stating the same idea and developing new beauties out of it, — especially when the variations are somewhat elaborate.

It must be remembered that mere repetition (even when modified, — as long as it can be proven to be nothing more than repetition) does not alter the form. A phrase, repeated, remains a phrase ; *nothing less than a decided alteration of the cadence itself* will transform it into a double-phrase (or period). Similarly, a period, repeated, remains a period, and does not become a double-period ; and a Part, repeated, remains the same Part. Therefore, the student will find it necessary to concentrate his attention upon these larger forms, and exercise both vigilance and discrimination in determining which sections of his design come under the head of " modified repetition."

For an illustration of the *repeated First Part*, see the 9th Song Without Words ; Part I is a four-measure period (of two small phrases) closing in the seventh measure ; the following four measures are its modified repetition. For an example of the *repeated Second and Third Parts*, see No. 48. In No. 29, both repetitions occur, with interesting changes ; the repetition of Part I begins in measure 13 ; that of Parts II and III in measure 35 ; the last 10 ½ measures are a coda.

The Five-part Form.   The repetition of the Second and Third Parts together is sometimes subjected to changes that are almost radical in their nature, and therefore appear to modify the form itself.   These important changes chiefly *affect the Second Part, when it reappears as " Fourth " Part.*   When the alteration of the Second Part (that is, the difference between Part IV and Part II) is sufficiently radical to suggest the presence of a virtually *new* Part, the design is called the Five-part Song-form.   The possible repetition of the First Part, it will be inferred, does not affect this distinction in the least; it hinges solely upon the treatment of the reproduction of *Part Two.*   For illustration :

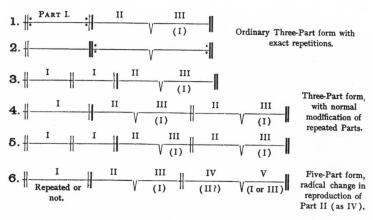

1. Ordinary Three-Part form with exact repetitions.

Three-Part form, with normal modification of repeated Parts.

Five-Part form, radical change in reproduction of Part II (as IV).

The Five-Part form is illustrated in the 14th Song Without Words ; — (first, number the measures ; observe that the two endings of Part I are to be counted as the *same measure,* and not separately ; they are both measure 8) : — Part I extends to the double-bar, and is repeated literally, only excepting the *rhythmic* modification of the final measure ; Part II extends from measure 9 to 23 ; Part III, measures 24–35 ; Part IV, measures 36–47 ; Part V, measures 48–60 ; coda to the end.   The comparison of Part IV with Part II discloses both agreement and diversity ;

they are, obviously, *practically the same Part*, but differ in key, in form, and in extent. The comparison of Parts I, III, and V reveals a similar condition, though the agreement here is much closer, and each confirms the leading statement.

A more characteristic example will be found in the familiar F major *Nachtstück* of Schumann, op. 23, No. 4, which see : — Part I extends from measure 2 to 9 (after 1 ½ measures of recitative introduction) ; Part II, measures 10–13 ; Part III, measures 14–21 ; Part IV, measures 22–32 ; Part V, measures 33–40 ; codetta to end. The Fourth Part bears very little resemblance to the Second, and assumes rather the character of a wholly independent Part.

Group of Parts. — In some, comparatively rare, instances, the arrangement of perfect cadences is such that, — coupled with independence of melodic formation and character, — the composition seems to separate into *four or more individual sections* or Parts, with or without a recurrence of the First one ; or into three *different* Parts, lacking the evidence of the return to the beginning. When such irregularities are encountered, or when any conditions appear which elude or baffle natural classification among the Three-Part Song-forms (simple or enlarged), the piece may be called a group of Parts. The use of this term is entirely legitimate, and is commended to the student on account of its convenience, for all examples of the Song-form which, *upon thoroughly conscientious analysis*, present confusing features, at variance with our adopted classification. Of one thing only he must assure himself, — that the design is a *Song-form* (*i.e.* an association of *Parts*), and not one of the larger forms to be explained in later chapters. The definition is given in Chapter IX (on page 84).

A fair illustration of the utility of the term " Group of Parts " is seen in Schumann, op. 68, No. 18. Others will be cited in the following Lesson.

Lesson 11. — Analyze the following examples of the enlarged Three-Part Song-form. As before, the form of each Part should be defined, and introductions and codas (if present) properly marked. All of the given examples belong to this chapter, but are not classified; it is purposely left to the student to determine where repetitions occur, and whether they are exact, or variated, — in a word, to decide which of the above diagrams the composition represents.

Mendelssohn, Songs Without Words, No. 3, No. 4, No. 8, No. 10, No. 11, No. 12, No. 16, No. 17, No. 19, No. 21, No. 23, No. 24, No. 27, No. 31, No. 34, No. 39, No. 43, No. 44, No. 46.

Schumann, op. 68, No. 5; No. 6; No. 10; No. 13; No. 15; No. 19; No. 22; No 30; No. 36; No. 43.

Mendelssohn, op. 72, No. 5.

Chopin, *Prelude*, op. 28, No. 17.

Mozart, pianoforte sonata No. 8, *Andante* (entire).

Mozart, No. 18, *Andantino* (of the " Fantasia ").

Chopin, *Mazurkas*, No. 1, No. 2, No. 4, No. 5, No. 8, No. 15, No. 16, No. 18, No. 37, No. 44, No. 48.

Groups of Parts :

Chopin, *Mazurkas*, No. 3 (apparently five Parts, not counting repetitions; Part V corroborates Part I, but the intervening sections are too independent to be regarded as one long Second Part, — as would be the case if this corroboration were Part III). Also No. 7 (same design); No. 14 (four Parts, the last like the first); No. 19 (four Parts, the fourth like the second) ; No. 20 ; No. 21 ; No. 27 (Part V like I, Part IV like II) ; No. 34 ; No. 39 ; No. 41.

Schubert, *Momens musicals*, op. 94, No. 3.

CHAPTER XII. THE SONG–FORM WITH TRIO.

Another method of enlargement consists in associating two different — though somewhat related — Song-Forms. The practice was so common in certain of the older dances, particularly in the minuet, that this design is also known as the *Minuet Form.*

The Principal Song. — The first division, called the principal song, is either a Two-Part or a Three-Part Song-form, — most commonly the latter. It is generally entirely complete in itself; the fact that another division is to be added, does not affect its character, form, or conception.

The " Trio," or Subordinate Song. — The division which follows, as second song-form, was formerly called the "Trio," and it has retained the name in the majority of examples of this form, although the old custom that gave rise to the term has long since been discontinued. A more accurate designation, and one that we shall here adopt, is "Subordinate Song." (Other names, which the student will encounter, are "maggiore," "minore," "intermezzo," "alternativo," etc.).

Like the principal song, its fellow (the subordinate song) may be either a Two-Part or a Three-Part design. It is very likely to resemble its principal song in species of measure, tempo, and general style; and its key may be the same as that of the principal division, or, at least, related to it. But similarity of style is by no means obligatory, the element of contrast having become more important than Unity, in a design of such extent. It is also usually complete in itself, though its connection with its principal song may involve a few measures of transitional material.

The "Da Capo." — This association of song-forms is subject to the principle which governs all tripartite forms, namely, the return to the beginning, and confirmation of the first (or principal) statement; not only because of the general desirability of such a return,

101

but because *the necessity for it increases with the growth of the form*. In a design that comprises a number of entire song-forms, it may be regarded as indispensable.

Therefore, the subordinate song is followed by a recurrence of the principal song, — called the *da capo* (or "from the beginning"), because of those Italian words of direction given to the player upon reaching the end of the "Trio," or subordinate song. The reproduction of the principal division is likely to be literal, so that the simple directions "*da capo*" suffice, instead of re-writing the entire division. But, here again, changes may be made, — generally unimportant variations which do not obscure the form ; or an abbreviation, or even slight extension. And a codetta or coda is sometimes added to the whole.

The Song with Trio is thus seen to correspond to the Three-Part Song-form, upon a larger scale. The several *Parts* of the latter become complete *Song-forms*. An important distinction, to which especial attention must be directed, is the *completeness* of the contents of each song-form, and their fairly distinct *separation* from each other, in the Song with Trio. The significance of these traits will become apparent to the analytic student, as he progresses along the line of form-evolution into the still larger designs.

Lesson 12. — The following examples all belong to the Song with Trio. They should be analyzed as usual, each Song separately, defining the Parts, their form, and other details, as minutely as possible. Careful analysis is the first condition of intelligent interpretation ; and the more complete the analysis, the fuller and more authoritative the interpretation : —

Beethoven, pianoforte sonatas : op. 2, No. 1, third movement ; the divisions are called *Menuetto* and *Trio*, therefore this is an authentic type of the present design ; each is a complete Three-Part Song-form ; the key is the same, though a change from minor into major takes place ; after the *Trio*, the *Menuetto* does not re-appear (on the printed page), but its reproduction is demanded by the words *Menuetto da capo*, at the end of the Trio.

Op. 2, No. 2, *Scherzo* and *Trio.*

Op. 2, No. 3, *Scherzo* and *Trio.*

Op. 7, third movement, *Allegro* and *Minore.*

Op. 10, No. 2, second movement, *Allegretto* (the subordinate song is not marked, but is easily distinguished; there are no *da capo* directions, because the principal song is re-written, with alterations).

Op. 10, No. 3, *Menuetto* and *Trio.*

Op. 14, No. 1, second movement, *Allegretto* and *Maggiore;* a coda is added.

Op. 22, *Menuetto* and *Minore.*

Op. 26, *Scherzo* and *Trio.*

Op. 27, No. 1, second movement, *Allegro molto;* the Trio is not marked; the "*da capo*" is variated, and a coda follows.

Op. 27, No. 2, *Allegretto* and *Trio.*

Op. 28, *Scherzo* and *Trio.*

Op. 31, No. 3, *Menuetto* and *Trio.*

Schumann, op. 68, No. 11; here there are no outward indications of the Song with Trio, but that is the design employed; for the subordinate song the measure is changed from 6–8 to 2–4, but the key remains the same; the reproduction of the principal song is indicated in German, instead of Italian.

No. 12, No. 29, No. 39 (here the *da capo* is considerably changed).

In No. 37 the "subordinate song" is represented by no more than a brief Interlude (measures 33–40) between the principal song and its recurrence, — just sufficient to provide an occasion for the latter (which, by the way, is also abbreviated).

Mozart, pianoforte sonatas: No. 2, *Andante cantabile;* each song-form has two Parts; the subordinate song changes into the minor.

No. 9, second movement, *Menuettos;* the subordinate song is marked "Menuetto II," a custom probably antedating the use of the word "Trio" (see Bach, 2d English Suite, *Bourrée* I and II).

No. 12, *Menuetto.*

Schubert, *Momens musicals,* op. 94, Nos. 1, 4, and 6.

Schumann, op. 82 (*Waldscenen*), Nos. 7 and 8.

Chopin, *Mazurkas,* Nos. 6, 12, 23, 47, 50. In Nos. 10, 45, 46 and 51, the subordinate song consists of *one* Part only, but is sufficiently distinct, complete, and separate to leave no doubt of the form.

Also Chopin, *Nocturne* No. 13 (op. 48, No. 1).

Examples of this compound Song-form will also be found, almost without exception, in Marches, Polonaises, and similar Dance-forms ; and in many pianoforte compositions of corresponding broader dimensions, which, *if extended beyond the very common limits of the Three-Part form,* will probably prove to be Song with Trio. This the student may verify by independent analysis of pianoforte literature, — never forgetting that uncertain examples may need (if small) to be classed among the group-forms, or (if large) may be suspected of belonging to the higher forms, not yet explained, and are therefore to be set aside for future analysis. Mention must be made of the fact that in some rare cases — as in Mendelssohn's well-known "Wedding March" — *two Trios,* and consequently two *da capos,* will be found.

CHAPTER XIII. THE FIRST RONDO–FORM.

Evolution. — It cannot have escaped the observant student of the foregoing pages, that the successive enlargement of the structural designs of musical composition is achieved by a process of natural growth and progressive evolution. No single form intrudes itself in an arbitrary or haphazard manner; each design emerges naturally and inevitably out of the preceding, in response to the necessity of expansion, and conformably with the same constant laws of unity and variety, — the active agents, along the entire unbroken line of continuous evolution, being *reproduction* (Unity) and legitimate *modification* (Variety) ; or, in other words, *modified repetition*. It is upon the indisputable evidence of such normal evolution in the system of musical structure, that our conviction of the legitimacy and permanence of this system rests.

The diagrams which appear on pages 78 and 98 partly illustrate the line of evolution, which, in its fullest significance, may be traced as follows : the *tone*, by the simplest process of reproduction, became a *figure ;* the figure, by multiplication or repetition, gave rise to the *motive ;* the latter, in the same manner, to the *phrase*. The repetition of the phrase, upon the infusion of a certain quality and degree of modification (chiefly affecting the cadences) became the *period ;* the latter, by the same process, became the double-period. The limit of coherent phrase-succession (without a determined interruption) being therewith reached, the larger Part-forms became necessary. The *Two-Part* form emerged out of the double-period, the two "connected" periods of which separated into two "independent" Parts, by the determined interruption in the center. And, be it well understood, each new design having once been thus established, its enlargement within its own peculiar boundaries followed as a matter of course ; I mean, simply, that the two Parts did not need to remain the *periods* that were their original type; the process of growth cannot be stopped. The *Three-Part* form resulted from adding to the Two-Part the perfecting reversion to the starting-point, and confirmation of the principal statement. The *Five-part* form, and the *Song with Trio* are enlargements of the Three-Part forms by repetition or multiplication; and with the latter the limit of this particular process appears to be achieved. Any further growth must take place from *within*, rather than by addition from without.

But the process of evolution continues steadily, as the student will witness. To one vital fact his attention is here called, — a fact which he is enjoined to hold in readiness for constant application, — namely, *that perfection of structural design is attained in the Three-Part form, and that every larger (or higher) form will have its type in this design, and its basis upon it.* The coming designs will prove to be expansions of the Three-Part form.

The Rondo-forms. — The structural basis of the Rondo, and other larger or (as they are sometimes called) higher forms, is the Subject or Theme. The form and contents of this factor, the Theme, are so variable that a precise definition can scarcely be given. It is a musical sentence of very distinct character, as concerns its melodic, harmonic and, particularly, its rhythmic consistency; and of sufficient length to establish this individuality, — seldom, if ever, less than an entire period or double-period; often a Two-Part, not infrequently a complete Three-Part Song-form, though never more than the latter.

In the Rondo-forms, two or three such Themes are associated in such *alternating succession that, after each new Theme, the first or Principal Theme recurs.* The term "Rondo" may be referred to this trait, the periodic return of the Principal theme, which, in thus "coming round" again, after each digression into another theme, imparts a characteristic circular movement (so to speak), to the design. In the rondos, then, all the movements of musical development revolve about one significant sentence or theme, the style of which therefore determines the prevailing character of the whole composition. This, which is naturally called the Principal theme, is placed at the beginning of the rondo. Its end being reached, it is temporarily abandoned for a second sentence, called the Subordinate theme, of more or less emphatically contrasting style and of nearly or quite equal length (generally shorter, however), and always in a different key. After this there occurs the momentous *return to the beginning,* — the most insistent and vital fundamental condition of good, clear, musical form, of whatsoever dimension or purport, — and the Principal theme reasserts itself, recurring with a certain degree of variation and elaboration (occasionally abbreviation), thus vindicating its title as *Principal* theme, and stamping its fellow-theme as a mere digression. After this, — if a still broader design is desired, — another digression may be made into a new Subordinate theme, in still another key, followed by the persistent return to the Principal theme. And so on. Upon the Subordinate theme, or themes, devolves the burden of variety and contrast, while the Principal theme fulfils the requirements of corroboration and concentration. A coda, sometimes of considerable length, is usually added ; it appears to be necessary, as a means of supplying an instinctive demand for balance, increased interest, and certain other scarcely definable conditions of very real importance in satisfactory music form.

Of the Rondo-forms there are three grades, distinguished respectively *by the number of digressions* from the Principal theme : —

The First Rondo-form, with one digression (or Subordinate theme), and one return to the Principal theme ;

The Second Rondo-form, with two digressions, and two returns ;

The Third Rondo-form, with three digressions and three returns.

The persistent recurrence of the Principal theme, something like a refrain, and the consequent regular alternation of the chief sentence with its contrasting subordinate sentences, are the distinctive structural features of the Rondo.

The First Rondo-form. — This consists, then, of a Principal theme (generally Two-Part or Three-Part Song-form) ; a Subordinate theme in a different key (probably a smaller form) ; a recurrence of the Principal theme (usually more or less modified or elaborated) ; and a coda.   Thus : —

Principal Theme.	*Subordinate Theme.*	*Prin. Theme.*	*Coda.*
2- or 3- Part Song-form. Probably a perfect cadence. Possibly a few beats or measures of transitional material, leading into next theme.	Period, Double-period, 2- or 3-Part form. Different style *and key.* Possibly a brief codetta ; and usually a few measures of Re-transition.	As before, usually variated. Sometimes abbreviated.	Optional.

The design is that of the tripartite forms.   But it is not to be confounded with the Three-Part *Song-form*, because at least one of its Themes, and probably both, will be a Part-form by itself.   It is an association of Song-forms, and therefore corresponds in design to the *Song with Trio.*   The first Rondo differs from the latter, however, in being more compact, more coherent and continuous, and more highly developed.   This manifests itself in the relation of the Themes to each other, which, despite external contrast, is more intimate than that between the Principal and Subordinate Song (or Trio) ; further, in the transitional passages from one Theme into the other (especially the Re-transition, or "returning passage ") ; in the customary elaboration of the recurring Principal Theme ; and in the almost indispensable coda, which often assumes considerable importance, and an elaborate form and character.

The evolution of the First Rondo-form of the Song with Trio may be clearly traced in classic literature.   Many intermediate stages appear, naturally ; and it is sometimes difficult to determine whether the design is Rondo or compound Song-form, simply because it is scarcely possible to decide just when the "Trio " assumes the more intimate relation of a Subordinate theme, or when the freedom and comparative looseness of association (peculiar to the Song with Trio) is transformed into the closer cohesion and greater smoothness of finish, *which fuses all the component Parts of the design into one compact whole,* — the distinctive stamp of all so-called " higher " forms.

The thoughtful examination and comparison of the following four examples will elucidate the matter : —

1. Beethoven, first pianoforte sonata (op. 2, No. 1), *Menuetto* and *Trio.* Already analyzed as a perfectly genuine Song with Trio.

2. Beethoven, pianoforte sonata, op. 28, second movement, *Andante.* The principal Song is in the Three-Part form, with exact repetitions. The subordinate song differs so radically in style, and each song is so complete and distinct from the other, that the form is almost certainly Song with Trio ; but there is a strong intimation of the Rondo-form in the elaborate variation of the *da capo,* and in the treatment of the coda (last 17 measures), in which motives from both Songs are associated so closely as to vindicate their kinship. In a word, this movement possesses, — despite the apparent independence of its Songs, — some degree of that continuity, compactness and artistic finish which culminate in the genuine Rondo-form.

3. Mozart, pianoforte sonata, No. 10, second movement (*Rondeau en polonaise*). The continuity and unity of this composition is so complete that it is certainly a Rondo-form ; the principal theme is a fairly large Three-Part form ; the subordinate theme (measure 47–69) is a Two-Part form, the second part corresponding in contents to the second Part of the principal theme ; the *recurrence* of the principal theme is abbreviated to one of its three Parts, and is merged in the coda (last seven measures), which assumes the nature of a mere extension. Despite all this evidence, there still remains a certain impression of structural independence, which, so to speak, betrays the " seams," and militates somewhat

against the spirit of the perfect Rondo-form.   See also, No. 13, *Adagio.*

4. Beethoven, pianoforte sonata, op. 2, No. 2, *Largo ;* the unessential details omitted in the following (in order to economize space) appear, of course, in the original, — to which the student is expected to refer.

PRINCIPAL THEME.   Three-Part Song-form.

PART III. Phrase, extended.

Cadence-measure. (as before.)

SUBOR-
Phrase I.

Perfect cadence.

DINATE THEME. Phrase-group.

Phrase 2 (three-measure).

Cad.

Phrase 3.

Cad.

PRINCIPAL THEME. As before, slightly modified.

Part I. Period-form.

This is a genuine First Rondo-form. All the factors of which it is composed, Phrases, Parts and Themes, are so closely inter-linked that the continuity, cohesion and *unity* of the whole is complete. The variety of contents which these factors exhibit (greatest, naturally, between the two themes), does not disturb the impression that the whole movement is a unit. This is due, at least partly, to the manner in which the perfect cadences are disguised; each one is passed over with the least possible check of rhythmic movement (measures 8, 19, etc.), thus snugly dove-tailing the structural factors. The coda is elaborate and unusually long; it consists of several "sections," as follows (see the original): from measure 1 (the last measure in Ex. 54) to measure 4, a phrase, derived from the second Part of the Principal theme; measures 5–7, an abbreviated repetition; measures 8–14, a phrase, derived from une Principal theme; measures 15–17, a transitional passage; measures 18–25, a period, closely resembling Part I of the Principal theme; measures 26–30, final phrase.

Lesson 13. — Analyze the following examples. They are not classified; the student must determine whether the form is pure First Rondo, or an intermediate grade between Rondo and "Song with Trio." One of the examples is a genuine Song with Trio; and one is a *Three-Part Song-form;* with reasonable vigilance the student will detect these "catches." To distinguish these three designs from each other, recollect —

That the Three-Part Song-form consists of three *single Parts*, fairly similar in character, fairly small in form, and severed either by a firm cadence, or by unmistakable proof of new "beginning;"

That in the first Rondo-form, at least one of the themes (if not both) contains *two* (or three) Parts; and,

That in the Song with Trio, the two "Songs" are more independent of each other, and more decisively separated, than are the "themes" of the Rondo-form.

With reference to all uncertain cases, it must be remembered that *the more doubtful a distinction is, the less important is its decision.* These designs naturally merge one in another, and at times it is folly to impose a definite analysis upon them.

The analysis should be as minute as possible, nevertheless The first step is to define the extremities of the two themes. This fixes the coda (and the introduction, if present) ; the re-transition (returning passage into the Principal theme) ; and the transition into the Subordinate theme — if present. The form of each theme must be defined in detail, as in Ex. 54 : —

Beethoven, pianoforte sonatas : op. 2, No. 1, *Adagio.*

Op. 7, *Largo.*

Op. 2, No. 3, *Adagio.*

Op. 79, *Andante.*

Op. 27, No. 1, *Allegro molto.*

Schubert, pianoforte *Impromptus,* op. 90, No. 2 ; and No. 3.

Chopin, *Mazurka,* No. 26.

Chopin, *Nocturnes :* op. 27, No. 1.

Op. 32, No. 2.

Op. 37, No. 1.

Op. 48, No. 1 ; and No. 2.

Op. 55, No. 1.

Op. 62, No. 1.

Op. 72, No. 1 (E minor, posthumous).

CHAPTER XIV. THE SECOND RONDO–FORM.

As described in the preceding chapter, the Second Rondo-form contains two digressions from the Principal theme, called respectively the first and second Subordinate themes. It bears the same relation to the Five-Part Song-form, that the First Rondo-form bears to the Three-Part Song-form.

For the sake of effective contrast, *the two Subordinate themes are generally differentiated* to a marked degree; more precisely stated, the *second* Subordinate theme is likely to differ strikingly both from the Principal theme and from the first Subordinate theme; the result is that, as a general rule, the second digression is more emphatic than the first.

To prevent the enlarged design from assuming too great dimensions, the several themes are apt to be more concise than in the first Rondo-form ; the Two-Part form is therefore more common than the Three-Part ; the first Subordinate theme is generally brief, and the Principal theme upon its recurrences, is frequently abbreviated, — especially the last one, which often merges in the coda.

An example of the second Rondo-form (which may be sufficiently illustrated without notes) will be found in the last movement of Beethoven's pianoforte sonata, op. 49, No. 2 (G major). Number the one hundred and twenty measures, and define the factors of the form with close reference to the following indications — the figures in parenthesis denoting the measures :

Principal theme, Part I (1–8), period-form ; Part II (9–12), phrase; Part III (13–20), period-form.

Transition, period-form (21–27), leading into the new key.

First Subordinate theme, period-form (28-36), with

Codetta, repeated (37-42).

Re-transition (43–47).

Principal theme, as before (48–67).

Second Subordinate theme, double-period (68–83) ; the process of *Re-transition* manifests its inception about one measure before (82), and is carried on to measure 87.

Principal theme, as before (88–107).

Coda, period, with modified repetition or consequent phrase (108–119), — followed by an extra perfect cadence, as extension.

Lesson 14. — Analyze the following examples, as usual. Review the directions given in Lesson 13 : —

Beethoven, pianoforte sonatas : op. 10, No. 3, last movement.

Op. 14, No. 2, last movement (called *Scherzo*).

Op. 79, last movement (very concise).

Op. 13, *Adagio* (still more concise. Is this not a Five-Part Song-form ?)

Beethoven, *Polonaise* for the pianoforte, op. 89.

Mozart, *Rondo* in A minor, for pianoforte.

CHAPTER XV. THE THIRD RONDO-FORM.

In this form of composition there are three digressions from the Principal theme. But, in order to avert the excess of variety, so imminent in a design of such length, the digressions are so planned that *the third one corresponds to the first.* That is, there are here again only two Subordinate themes (as in the Second Rondo-form), which alternate with each other, so that the succession of thematic factors is as follows: Principal Theme; 1st Subordinate Theme; Principal Theme; 2d Subordinate Theme; Principal Theme; 1st Subordinate Theme; Principal Theme; and coda.

It will be observed that this arrangement is another confirmation and embodiment of the Three-Part (tripartite) form, with its "recurrence of the first section," magnified into larger proportions than any examples thus far seen. The three portions are called *Divisions.* The first is known as the *Exposition,* comprising the Principal Theme, First Subordinate Theme, and recurrence of the Principal Theme; the second division consists of the Second Subordinate Theme only; the Third Division is the *Recapitulation* of the first Division.

The Exposition. — This first Division, the "statement," compounded of two themes and a recurrence, is in itself a complete (though probably very concise) First Rondo-form; therefore, in order to confirm the intended design, at least one of its themes must contain two (or more) Parts, — otherwise it would be no more, all together, than a Three-Part Song-form, and the *whole* Rondo would be reduced to the design of the First Rondo-form. In a word, the Exposition must correspond concisely to the table given on page 108. The First Subordinate theme takes its usual emphatic position in a different key, — generally closely related to the key of the Principal theme.

Sometimes, but by no means regularly, the **Exposition closes** with a decisive perfect cadence in the original key.

The Middle Division. — As this should balance (at least approximately, the Exposition, it is likely to be a fairly broad design, — not greater, however, than a Three-Part Song-form (possibly with repetitions), and often no more than a Two-Part form. As intimated in the preceding chapter, the Second Subordinate theme is usually strongly contrasted with the other themes, in character, key, and length ; but the same unity of total effect is necessary, as in the smaller Rondo-forms. The re-transition (or returning passage) is often quite lengthy and elaborate ; it is seldom an independent section of the form, however, but generally developed out of the last phrase of the theme, by the process of "dissolution," — to be explained more fully in Chapter XVII.

The Recapitulation. — This corresponds, theoretically, to the *da capo* in the Song with Trio, or to the variated recurrence of the Principal theme in the First Rondo-form. But it is more than either of these. The term "Recapitulation" is more comprehensive than " recurrence " (in the sense in which we have thus far employed the latter word), as it always refers to the reproduction of a *collection* of themes, and, chiefly on this account, is subject to certain specific conditions of technical treatment.

Recapitulation, in the larger designs of composition, *invariably involves transposition*, or change of key, — the transposition of the First Subordinate theme, from the key chosen for its first announcement (in the Exposition) back *to the principal key* of the piece. This, as may be inferred, greatly affects the original transition and re-transition ; and it may necessitate changes within the theme itself, in consequence of the change of register.

Further, the last recurrence of the Principal theme being no less than its fourth announcement, is rarely complete ; as a rule, a brief intimation (the first motive or phrase) is deemed sufficient, and this is then dissolved into the coda ; or the Principal theme, as such, is omitted, or affiliated with the coda, or one of its sections.

For an illustration of the Third Rondo-form, the student is referred to the last movement of Beethoven's pianoforte sonata, op. 2, No. 2, the diagram of which is as follows : —

Exposition.			*Middle Division.*	*Recapitulation.*		
Pr. Th.	1st Sub. Th.	Pr. Th.	2d Sub. Th.	Pr. Th.	1st Sub. Th.	Pr. Th. and Coda
A maj.	E maj.	A maj.	A minor	A maj.	A maj.	A maj.

For its detailed analysis, number the measures as usual (there are 187, the "second ending" not being counted), and define each factor of the form by reference to the given indications, — the figures in parenthesis again denoting the measures : —

Principal Theme, Part I (1–8), period-form. Part II (9–12), phrase. Part III (13–16), phrase.

Transition, period-form (17–26), leading into the new key.

First Sub. Theme, period, Antecedent (27–32), Consequent (33–39).

Re-transition (40).

Principal Theme, as before, (41–56). This ends the **Exposition**.

Second Sub. Theme, Part I (57–66), period, literal repetition. Part II (67–74) period-form. Part III (75–79) phrase.

Parts II and III repeated (80–92) ; the process of *re-transition* begins one measure earlier (91), and is pursued to measure 99.

The **Recapitulation** begins in the next measure with the

Principal Theme, as before, slightly modified (100–115).

Transition, as before, slightly abbreviated (116–123).

First Subordinate Theme, as before, but transposed to the principal key, A major, and somewhat modified (124–135).

Principal Theme begins in measure 135, where the preceding theme ends ; consequently, there is an Elision. In measure 140 it is dissolved into the

Coda : Section 1 (to measure 148).

Section 2 (149–160).

Section 3 (161–172).

Section 4 (173–180).

Section 5 (to end).

Lesson 15. — Analyze the following examples, as usual. They represent chiefly the Third Rondo-form, but *one example each* of the First and Second Rondo-forms have been introduced, to stimulate the vigilance of the student. Review the directions given in Lesson 13:

Beethoven, pianoforte sonatas : op. 26, last movement, (very concise, but a perfect model of the form).

Op. 28, last movement.

Op. 7, last movement.

Op. 2, No. 3, last movement.

Op. 13, last movement.

Op. 22, last movement.

Op. 14, No. 1, last movement.

Op. 31, No. 1, *Adagio.*

Beethoven, *Rondos* for pianoforte, op. 51, No. 1 ; and op. 51, No. 2.

Mozart, pianoforte sonata, No. 4, last movement ; No. 3, last movement.

CHAPTER XVI. THE SONATINE FORM.

Classification of the Larger Forms. — The Sonatine form is the smaller variety of two practically kindred designs, known collectively as the Sonata-allegro forms. In order to obtain a clear conception of its relation to the latter, and also to the Rondo-forms, it is necessary to subject the entire group of so-called "higher" forms to a brief comparison.

The larger, broader, or "higher" designs of musical composition are divided into two classes: the three *Rondo-forms*, and the two *Sonata-allegro forms*. The latter constitute the superior of the two classes, for the following reasons : —

In the first place, the rondos rest upon a narrower thematic basis, centering in one single theme — the Principal one — about which the other themes revolve. Further, their most salient structural feature is nothing more significant than simple *alternation* (of the Principal theme with its one or more Subordinates) the Principal theme recurs after each digression with a persistence that lends a certain one-sidedness to the form, — only excepting in the Third (and highest) Rondo-form, which, by virtue of its broad Recapitulation of the first Division, approaches most nearly the rank of the Sonata-allegro design, as will be seen.

In the Sonata-allegro forms, on the other hand, the leading purpose is *to unite two co-ordinate themes upon an equal footing ;* one is to appear as often as the other ; and the two themes *together* constitute the thematic basis of the design. These are, as in the rondos, a Principal theme (called principal because it appears first, and thus becomes in a sense the index of the whole movement), and a Subordinate theme (so called in contradistinction to the other), — contrasting in character, as usual, but actually of equal importance, and of nearly or quite equal length. To these, there is commonly added a codetta (or "concluding theme" as it is

121

sometimes called, though it seldom attains to the dignity of a *theme*), — sometimes two, or even more, codettas, which answer the general purpose of a coda, rounding off and balancing this Division of the design. This union of the two or three thematic components that are to represent the contents of the design, is the *Exposition*, or first Division, of the Sonata-allegro forms. It indicates a point of contact between the latter and the rondo, — in the *Third* form of which we also find an Exposition. Careful comparison of the two types of exposition reveals the significant difference between the two classes, however ; in the Third Rondo, the exposition was an *alternation* of themes, with decided preference for the principal one ; in the Sonata-allegro it is a *union* of themes, without preference, resulting in a broader thematic basis.

The Sonatine Form. — In the Sonatine-form, or the smaller variety of the sonata-allegro designs, this Exposition (or first Division) is followed *at once*, — or after a few measures of interlude, or re-transitional material, — by a Recapitulation of the Division, as was seen in the Third Rondo-form, and under the same conditions of transposition as there. The diagram of the form is therefore as follows : —

Exposition.			*Very*	*Recapitulation*		
PR. TH.	SUB. TH.	CODETTA.	*brief*	PR. TH.	SUB. TH.	CODETTA.
As usual.	In some related key.	Optional.	*Interlude.*	As before.	In the principal key.	Also in principal key.

An additional coda is, as usual, likely to appear at the end.

This diagram should be very carefully compared with that of the Third Rondo-form on page 119, and the points both of agreement and dissimilarity noted. More minute details of the Sonatine form will be given in the next chapter, in connection with the larger and more fully developed Sonata-allegro form.

An illustration of the Sonatine-form will be found in Mozart, 6th pianoforte sonata, *adagio*. Number the measures, as usual, and analyze with reference to the indications given ; the figures in parenthesis again denote the measures.

Principal Theme, B-flat major, period-form, — possibly double-period, because of the slow tempo and large measures (1–8). There is no Transition.

Subordinate Theme, F major, period-form, extended. Antecedent (9–12); consequent, very similar (13–16); extension by addition of new phrase, as in the group-form (16½–19).

Codetta, also in F major, very brief, only one-half measure, and repeated as usual (19½ –20). This ends the **Exposition.**

Interlude, the remaining beats of measure 20; it is, of course, a brief re-transition, and is therefore strongly suggestive of the First Rondo-form, the *details of which exactly coincide, thus far, with the above factors of the sonatine-form.* Such coincidences merely confirm the unbroken line of evolution, and are to be expected in the system of legitimate, rational music designs. The **Recapitulation** (the original *da capo*) follows, beginning with the

Principal Theme, B-flat major, as before (21–28) but somewhat embellished. Again, there is no Transition. (Here the similarity to the First Rondo ends.)

Subordinate Theme, corresponds very closely to the former version, but transposed to B-flat major, the principal key, and variated (29–39).

Codetta, also in B-flat major (39½–40), slightly extended. There is no coda.

Lesson 16. — Analyze the following examples of the sonatine-form, in the usual exhaustive manner : —

Beethoven, pianoforte sonatas : op. 10, No. 1, *Adagio.*

Op. 31, No. 2, *Adagio.*

Mendelssohn, *Andante cantabile* in B-flat major (pianoforte).

Mozart, pianoforte sonata, No. 17, *Andante amoroso* (somewhat longer interlude).

Mendelssohn, *Presto agitato* in B minor for pianoforte (preceded by an "Andante cantabile" which has no connection with the sonatine-form of the *presto*, but may also be analyzed). This design is very broad ; each factor is expanded to its fullest legitimate extent, especially the "codetta" section.

CHAPTER XVII. THE SONATA–ALLEGRO FORM.

Origin of the Name. — The fully developed Sonata-allegro form is the design in which the classic overture and the first movement of the symphony, sonata and concerto are usually framed. The student must be careful not to confound this musical form with the *complete* sonata of three or four movements. It is not to be called the "sonata form," but the "sonata-allegro form." It is to one movement only, generally the first one, which is (or was) very commonly an *allegro* tempo in the sonata and symphony, that the present design refers; and its name, sonata-allegro, is derived from that old historic species of the sonata which consisted originally of but one movement, generally an *allegro*.

The Sonata-Allegro Form. — As distinguished from the sonatine-form, with its two Divisions, this larger species, based upon precisely the same structural idea, has *three Divisions*, — the Exposition, a middle Division called the Development (growing out of the brief interlude of the sonatine-form), and the Recapitulation. The diagram (the keys of which correspond to the plan of Beethoven, op. 14, No. 2, first movement) is as follows : —

Exposition.			*Middle Div.*	*Recapitulation.*		
Pr. Th.	Sub. Th.	Codetta.	*Development, various keys, ending with Retransition.*	Phr. Th.	Sub. Th.	Codetta and Coda.
G maj.	D maj.	D maj.		G maj.	G maj.	G maj.

Compare this diagram, also, with that of the Third Rondo-form, and note, accurately, the points of resemblance and contrast.

Compare it, further, with the diagram of the sonatine-form, on page 122. It will be observed that here the Recapitulation does not follow the Exposition at once, as there, but that a complete middle division intervenes, instead of the brief interlude or re-tran sition; from which the student may conclude that the sonatine-form gradually grows into the sonata-allegro form, as this interlude becomes longer, more elaborate, and more like an independent division of the design.   Or inversely, and perhaps more correctly, the sonata-allegro becomes a sonatine-design *by the omission (or contraction) of the middle Division.*

The Exposition. — The presentation of the thematic factors, the statement or Exposition of the two themes and codetta, is made exactly as in the sonatine-form, though probably upon a broader scale.   The Principal theme is usually a Two-Part Song-form, at least; often Three-Part.   In broader designs, a separate transitional passage appears; in more concise designs, the transition is developed out of the last Part of the Principal theme by the process of dissolution — as will be seen.   The object of the transition is, as usual, *to lead into the new key* (of the Subordinate theme). It is sometimes, though very rarely, omitted.

The Subordinate theme contrasts notably with its fellow, but asserts equal importance, as a rule, and may be of equal, or nearly equal, length.   The addition of a codetta is almost indispensable, and frequently two or more appear, growing successively shorter, and generally repeated.   In the sonata-allegro *the Exposition closes, as a rule, with a very decisive perfect cadence,* followed by a double-bar, and — especially in older sonatas — repetition-marks; the repetition of the Exposition being justly considered important, as a means of emphasizing the "statement," and enforcing the hearer's attention to the thematic contents before proceding to their development in the second division of the form.   In the sonatine-form, on the contrary, this positive termination of the Exposition (and consequently the double-bar and repetition) will very rarely be found.

The Development, or Middle Division.   The second division of the sonata-allegro form is devoted to a more or less extensive and elaborate manipulation and combination of such figures, motives, phrases or Parts of the Exposition as prove inviting and convenient for the purpose, or challenge the imaginative faculty of the composer. In this division, opportunity is provided for the exhibition of technical skill, imagination and emotional passion ; for the creation of ingenious contrasts and climaxes, and, in a word, for the development of unexpected resources not strikingly manifest in the more sober presentation of the thematic factors during the Exposition. The intermingling of *new material* is naturally also involved in the process of development ; sometimes to such an extent that the new predominates over the old, — in which case the middle Division is more properly called an **Episode.**

This second Division of the sonata-allegro form (the Development or Episode) corresponds precisely, as will be recognized, to the second Part of the Three-Part Song-form ; consequently, it represents the "departure" (see page 90), and entails, in rational form, the significant "return" to the beginning. Further, it matches to some degree the "digression" in the rondo-forms. At all events, its important structural function is to establish contrast ; and the necessity for corroboration of the leading thematic ideas — in consequence of this contrast — is satisfied in the Division which succeeds.

It is sometimes possible to mark the exact point where the Development ends and the process of re-transition commences ; but usually the return to the beginning is accomplished so gradually that no sensible interruption occurs.

The Recapitulation. — This, the third Division, is, as usual, a review of the original presentation of the thematic material, — the recurrence of the Exposition. It is sometimes a nearly exact reproduction, *excepting the necessary change of key in the Subordinate theme and codetta,* and such modification of the transitional section as may be thereby involved. Sometimes, however, considerable alteration is made, at times so elaborate (especially in broader examples) that, though preserving easy recognizability, the Recapitulation assumes the appearance of a new version of the Exposition, and becomes a more independent part of the design.

A *coda* is almost always added; sometimes brief, but occasionally so elaborate and extensive as to merit the appellation " second
Development."

Dissolution. — When any section of a higher form starts out
with a perfectly definite structural intention, pursues this intention
for a time (sufficient to establish it), but then insensibly diverges
and gradually adopts a new modulatory direction, — as transition
into the following section, — the form is said to be dissolved.
Such dissolution takes place, naturally, within the *later* section of
the theme, or Part, or whatever it may be, whose actual, definite
ending in the expected key is thus frustrated.   For instance, the
second (or third) Part of a theme may be dissolved; or the last
phrase of a period or double-period; or the repetition of a phrase.
And the dissolution is invariably applied before a transition or
re-transition, as a means of interlocking the factors of the form
more closely and coherently.   Therefore it is a process peculiarly
adapted to the higher designs of composition, and is seldom omitted
in the sonata-allegro form.   For an illustration, see Beethoven's
sonata, op. 14, No. 2, first movement : The Principal theme is a
Two-Part Song-form ; Part I, a period, from measures 1 to 8 ;
Part II begins in measure 9, and has every appearance of becom-
ing also a period ; its Antecedent phrase closes in measure 12, its
Consequent begins in measure 13 — but its end, *as Second Part*,
in the usual definite manner, cannot be indicated ; the key is
quietly changed from G to D, and then to A, in obedience to the
call of the Subordinate theme (beginning in measure 26), into
which these last 10 or 12 measures have evidently been a Transition.   The Second Part of the Principal theme therefore includes
the transition ; but where the Second Part (as such) ends, and the
transition (as such) begins, it is impossible to point out accurately.
The definition of this Principal theme is, " Two-Part form with
dissolved Second Part," or, still better, " *with transitional Second
Part.*"

*   *   *

In our illustration of the sonata-allegro form it is necessary, on account of limited space, to select a very concise example, of unusual brevity, — Beethoven, sonata, op. 49, No. 1, first movement ; the original may be referred to, for the omitted details : —

EXPOSITION.

PRINCIPAL THEME (Double-period, dissolved).

Consequent, repeated, beginning with second measure.

CODETTA (2-meas. phrase).

Perf. cad.

Repetition.

DEVELOPMENT (OR EPISODE).
First section (from subord. theme).

Second section (new).

Repetition.

Third Section (from Codetta).

RECAPITULATION.

PRINCIPAL THEME (Double-period.)

SUBORDINATE THEME (extended

The thematic factors are small, but none is omitted ; every essential component is represented.

For a more extended and fully developed example of the sonata-allegro form, see Beethoven, pianoforte sonata, op. 14, No. 2, first movement ; number the 200 measures, and verify all the details according to the following analysis (figures in parenthesis refer as usual to the measures) : —

Principal Theme, Part I, period-form (1–8).   Part II (9–), dissolved (about 14) into *Transition* (–25).

Subordinate Theme, Part I, period, extended (26–36).   Part II, period, probably (37–41–47).

Codetta I, period, extended (48–58).

Codetta II, Small phrase, extended (59–63).   Here the Exposition closes, with the customary double-bar and repetition marks.

Development, Section 1 (64–73), from Principal theme.   Section 2 (74–80), from Subordinate theme.   Section 3 (81–98), from Principal theme.   Section 4 (99–107), closely resembling the Principal theme, but in a remote key.   This section practically ends the Development, inasmuch as it culminates upon the *dominant of the original key.*   Section 5 (107–115), establishment of the dominant.   Section 6 (115–124), the *Re-transition.*   The *Recapitulation* begins with the

Principal Theme, Part I, period (125–132).   Part II, group of phrases, longer than before (133–152).

Subordinate Theme, as before, but in the principal key (153–174).

Codetta (I), as before, but slightly extended (175–187).   The second codetta is omitted.

Coda, phrase, repeated and extended (188–200).

Relation to the Three-Part Song-form. — In a former chapter (XIII) the Three-Part form was defined as the type of perfect structural design, upon which every larger (or higher) form is based.   Nowhere is the connection more striking, and the process of natural evolution out of this germ more directly apparent, than in the sonata-allegro design.   See the diagram on page 124.   The Exposition corresponds to the First Part, *so expanded as to comprise the two themes and codetta,* fused into one larger division; the "statement" of a more comprehensive thematic group than the ordinary Part contains, but no more, for all that, than the usual initial "statement."   The Development corresponds to the Second

Part (proportionately expanded), and the Recapitulation to the Third Part, or recurrence and confirmation of the "statement."

Any Three-Part Song-form, the moment that its First Part expands and divides into the semblance of two fairly distinct thematic sections, becomes what might be called a miniature sonata-allegro form. Many Three-Part Song-forms are so broad. and many sonata-allegros so diminutive, that it is here again often difficult to determine the line of demarcation between them. Example 55 (cited because of its comparative brevity) is scarcely more than such a broadly expanded Three-Part Song-form. An example which approaches much more nearly the unmistakable Three-Part song, may be found in Mozart, sonata No. 12, *Menuetto :* —

Part I, section one (embryo of a principal theme), measures 1–10, period, extended;˙ section two (embryo of a subordinate theme) measures 11–18, period, *in different key.*

Part II, group of three phrases, measures 19–30.

Part III, section one, as before, measures 31–40; section two. as before, *but in the principal key*, measures 41–48.

This is, of course, a Three-Part Song-form; but the essential features of the Sonata-allegro are unquestionably present, in miniature.

See also, Beethoven, sonata, op. 101, first movement ; certainly a sonata-allegro design, but diminutive.

* * *

The superiority of the sonata-allegro form over all other musical designs, is amply vindicated by the breadth of its thematic basis, the straightforwardness and continuity of its structural purpose, the perfection of its thematic arrangement, and the unexcelled provision which it affords for unity, contrast, corroboration, balance, and whatever else a thoroughly satisfactory structural design seems to demand. Hence, while brief triumphs of apparent "originality" may be achieved by simply running counter to this and similar designs, it seems scarcely possible that any musical form could be contrived that would surpass the sonata-allegro, the last and highest of the forms of composition.

Lesson 17. — Analyze the following examples, as usual, carefully defining all the details of the form, according to the general plan adopted in our text : —

Beethoven, pianoforte sonatas; op. 2, No. 1, first movement (diminutive, but very complete and perfect).

Op. 2, No. 2, first movement.

Op. 10, No. 3, *Largo.*

Op. 22, first movement (four or five codettas).

Op. 14, No. 1, first movement.

Op. 22. *Adagio.*

Op. 27, No. 2, last movement.

Op. 28, first movement.

Op. 31, No. 1, first movement.

Op. 31, No. 3, first movement (the last 2½ measures of the Exposition are a transitional Interlude, which leads back into the repetition, and on into the Development).

Same sonata, *Scherzo.*

Op. 31, No. 2, last movement (coda contains the entire principal theme).

Op. 78, first movement (diminutive).

Op. 79, first movement.

Op. 90, first movement, (no "double-bar").

Op. 57, first movement.

Same sonata, last movement.

Mozart, sonatas : No. 7, first movement.

No. 3, first movement.   No. 4, first movement ; also *Andante.*

No. 8, first movement.   No. 5, first movement.

No. 10, first movement.   No. 6, first movement.

No. 1, *Andante.*   No. 6, last movement.

Mendelssohn, pianoforte *Caprice,* op. 33, No. 2 (brief introduction).

Sonata, op. 6, first movement.

Op. 7, No. 7.

Fantasia, op. 28, last movement.

Schubert, pianoforte sonatas : op. 143, first movement.

Op. 42, first movement.

Op. 120, first movement.

Op. 147, first movement (in the Recapitulation, the principal theme is transposed).

Op. 164, first movement (the same).

Beethoven, symphony, No. 5, first movement.

Symphony, No. 1, first *Allegro ;* also the second movement ; and the *Finale.*

CHAPTER XVIII. IRREGULAR FORMS.

Causes. — Despite the many points of resemblance between the various forms to which our successive chapters have been devoted, — the natural consequence of a continuous line of structural evolution to which each plan owes its origin, — they are separate and independent designs, with individual character and purpose ; so much so, that the composer may, and usually does, select and apply his form according to the purpose which he has in view. But the form is made for the music, not the music for the form ; no serious composer writes music for the sake of the form, but chooses the form merely as a means to an end.   The highest ideal of structural dignity and fitness is, to work from the thematic germ *outward*, and to let the development of this germ, *the musical contents*, determine and justify the structural plan and arrangement.

But the aims of the composer outnumber the regular forms, and therefore modifications are unavoidable, in order to preserve the latitude which perfect freedom of expression demands.   The student may rest assured of the existence of many irregular species of these fundamental forms (as exceptions to the rule) and must expect to encounter no little difficulty and uncertainty in defining the class to which his example belongs, — until wider experience shall have made him expert.

All such irregular (or, in a sense, intermediate) varieties of form must necessarily either admit of demonstration as modification of the regular designs ; or they will evade demonstration altogether, as lacking those elements of logical coherence which constitute the vital and only condition of "form and order" in musical composition.

To these latter comparatively "*formless*" designs belong : — all the group-forms ; the majority of fantasias, the potpourri, and, as a rule, all so-called tone-poems, and descriptive (program) music generally.

On the other hand, those irregular designs which nevertheless admit of analysis according to the fundamental principles of structural logic, and are therefore directly referable to one or another of the regular forms, may be classified in the following four-fold manner — as Augmentation, Abbreviation, Dislocation, or Mixture, of the proximate fundamental design.

1. **Augmentation of the Regular Form.** — To this species belong those forms (small and large) which are provided with a separate Introduction, or Interludes, or an *independent* Coda (in addition to, or instead of, the usual consistent coda).

For example, Beethoven, pianoforte sonata, op. 13, first movement; the first ten measures (*Grave*) are a wholly independent Introduction, in phrase-group form, with no other relation to the following than that of key, and no connection with the fundamental design excepting that of an extra, superfluous, member. The principal theme of the movement (which is a sonata-allegro) begins with the *Allegro di molto*, in the 11th measure. Similar superfluous sections, derived from this Introduction, reappear as Interlude between the Exposition and Development, and near the end, as independent sections of the coda.

In a manner closely analogous to that just seen, the fundamental design of any movement in a *concerto* is usually expanded by the addition of periodically recurring sections, called the "*tutti*-passages," and by a "*cadenza*," occurring generally within the regular coda. In some concerto-allegros (for instance, in the classic forms of Mozart, Beethoven and others), the first orchestral *tutti* is a complete *introductory* Exposition, in concise form, of the thematic material used in the body of the movement. See the first pianoforte concerto of Beethoven, first movement.

Further, when the design is one of unusual breadth, as in some symphonic movements, or in elaborate chamber music, the number of fundamental thematic members may be so multiplied that it is necessary to assume the presence of *two successive Subordinate themes,* of equal independent significance, — such significance that neither of them could be confounded with a mere codetta, or any other inferior thematic member. See Beethoven, pianoforte sonata, op. 7, first movement; the Subordinate theme runs from measure 41 to 59; it is followed by another thematic section (60–93) which is so independent, important and lengthy, that it evidently ranks coördinate with the former, as *second Subordinate theme.* It might, it is true, be called the second Part of the Subordinate theme (the latter being no more than a repeated period) ; or it might be regarded as the first codetta ; its thematic independence seems, however, to stamp it Second Subordinate theme.

Further, it is not uncommon to extend the sonatine-form by adding, at the end, a more or less complete recurrence of the Principal theme, — instead of, or dissolved into, the customary coda. This may be seen in Mozart, pianoforte sonata, No. 3, *Andantino;* the superfluous recurrence of the Principal theme begins in measure 19 from the end, after the regular sonatine-design has been achieved, fully, though concisely.

2. **Abbreviation of the Regular Form**. — This consists chiefly in the omission of the Principal theme after the Development (that is, in beginning the Recapitulation with the Subordinate theme). Other contractions, by omission of *portions* (Parts) of important thematic members, during the Recapitulation, are also possible, but not so common.

An illustration of the omitted Principal theme may be found in Mendelssohn, Songs Without Words, No. 5 : —

Principal Theme, period, extended (measures 1–11, dissolved into Transition — 18).

Subordinate Theme, phrase, repeated and extended (19–28). *Codetta* (28–33). *Double-bar.*

Development (measures 34–58). *Retransition* (59–62).

Principal Theme — omitted.

Subordinate Theme, as before (63–76). *Codetta.*

3. **Dislocation of Thematic Members.** — By this is meant, any exchange or alteration of the regular and expected arrangement of members. This can refer, naturally, only to what occurs *after the Exposition,* — that is, during the Recapitulation; for it is the Exposition which determines the plan, and regular order, of the thematic members. For example, Mozart, pianoforte sonata, No. 13, first movement : —

Principal Theme, with *Transition* (measures 1–27).
Subordinate Theme (28–41).
Codetta I (42–53).
Codetta II (54–58). In the Recapitulation, the arrangement is thus : —

Principal Theme, Codetta I, Subordinate Theme, Codetta II ; that is, the first codetta appears before, instead of after, the Subordinate theme.

4. **Mixture of Characteristic Traits.** — This process tends to affiliate the two distinct classes of larger or higher forms, whose respective characteristics were explained and compared at the beginning of Chapter XVI. Upon very careful revision of this explanation, and reference to the given diagrams, the student will perceive that the distinctive trait of the sonata-allegro form is the section of *Development* which it contains; and that of the three Rondo-forms is the absence of such a Development. Of the mixed forms under consideration there are two: one in which a section of Development is introduced into the Rondo (as substitute for one of its Subordinate themes); and the other a sonata-allegro, in which the Development is omitted, and a new theme (a sort of additional Subordinate theme) inserted in its place. In other words, a Rondo (second or third form — probably *not* the first rondo-form) with a Development; and a sonata-allegro with a new Middle theme, or Episode (as we have already called it).

The Rondo with Development is illustrated in Beethoven, pianoforte sonata, op. 27, No. 1, last movement; it is the third rondo-form, designed as follows : —

Principal Theme, Two-Part form (measures 1–24).

Transition (25–35).

First Subordinate Theme, period, extended,— or phrase-group (36–56).   *Codetta* (57–72).

Re-transition (73–81).

Principal Theme (82–97).

Transition (98–106).   Then, instead of the Second Subordinate theme, a

Development (106–138); followed by an elaborate

Re-transition (139–166), and a regular

Recapitulation.   Two wholly independent coda-sections are added, an *Adagio* (derived from the third movement of the sonata) and a *Presto*, based upon the Principal theme.

The sonata-allegro with new Middle theme is illustrated in Beethoven, pianoforte sonata, op. 14, No. 1., first movement; the middle Division contains a preliminary allusion to the Principal theme, but is otherwise an entirely new thematic member, very suggestive of the "Second Subordinate theme" of the Rondos (17 measures long, — up to the Re-transition, in which, again, the Principal theme is utilized).

Lesson 18. — Analyze the following examples of Irregular form. They are classified, as in the text :

1. Beethoven, sonata, op. 81, first movement.

Beethoven, sonata, op. 49, No. 2, first movement.

Beethoven, sonata, op. 2, No. 3, first movement.

Beethoven, sonata, op. 49, No. 1, last movement (*not* "Rondo," as marked, but sonatine-form, augmented).

Mozart, sonata No. 1, first movement.

Mozart, sonata No. 17, last movement (Rondo, with three Subordinate themes).

Mendelssohn, *Capriccio brillant*, in B minor.

Schubert, pianoforte sonata No. 8 (Peters ed.), *Adagio.*

2. Mendelssohn, *Præludium*, op. 35, No. 3.

Mozart, sonata No. 8, last movement.

Schubert, sonata No. 8, last movement.

Brahms, pianoforte *Capriccio*, op. 116, No. 1.

Chopin, pianoforte sonata, op. 35, first movement.

3. Mozart, sonata No. 3, first movement.

Mozart, sonata No. 13, last movement (the Development occurs *after* instead of before the Principal theme, — in the Recapitulation).

4. Beethoven, pianoforte sonata, op. 31, No. 1, last movement.

Beethoven, pianoforte sonata, op. 90, last movement.

Mendelssohn, pianoforte étude, op. 104, No. 2.

Beethoven, pianoforte sonata, op. 10, No. 1, first movement.

Beethoven, pianoforte sonata, op. 2, No. 1, last movement.

Mozart, sonata No. 7, *Andante*.

Mozart, sonata No. 14, last movement.

CHAPTER XIX. APPLICATION OF THE FORMS.

THE use of the various forms of composition, that is, their selection with a view to general fitness for the composer's object, is, primarily, simply a question of length. The higher æsthetic law of adjusting the design to the contents, of which we spoke in the preceding chapter, comes into action after the main choice has been determined.

The smallest complete form, that of the **Phrase,** can scarcely be expected to suffice for an independent piece of music, though its occurrence as independent *section* of an entire composition is by no means rare. The nearest approach to the former dignity is the use of the Large phrase in one instance by Beethoven, as theme for his well-known pianoforte Variations in C minor; this theme, and consequently each variation, is a complete and practically independent composition. At the beginning of Beethoven's pianoforte sonata, Op. 27, No. 1, the student will find a succession of independent four-measure phrases, each with a definite perfect cadence, and therefore complete in itself; this chain of independent phrases is, in fact, the structural basis of the entire first movement, interrupted but briefly by the contrasting *Allegro*. The simple phrase may, also, find occasional application in brief exercises for song or piano; and we have witnessed its use as introduction, and as codetta, in many of the larger designs.

The next larger complete form, the **Period,** is somewhat more likely to be chosen for an entire composition, but by no means frequently. The early grades of technical exercises (public-school music, and similar phases of elementary instruction) are commonly written in period-form. and some of the smallest complete songs in literature (a few of Schumann's, Schubert's, and others) may be defined as period-forms, extended. The theme of the Chaconne (found in the works of Handel, Bach, and even some modern writers) is usually a period. Of the Préludes of Chopin for pianoforte (op. 28), at least four do not exceed the design of the extended period. But these are, naturally, exceptional cases ; the proper function of the period-form in music is, to represent the *Parts*, and other fairly complete and independent thematic members of larger forms. This is very largely true of the **Double-period,** also ; though it is a very appropriate and common design for the hymn-tune, and similar vocal compositions ; and is somewhat more likely to appear as complete composition (in exercises, smaller piano pieces and songs) than is the single period. Nine of Chopin's Préludes are double-periods.

The **Two-Part Song-form,** as already intimated, is not as common as might be supposed. It is sometimes employed in smaller compositions for piano (variation-themes and the like), or voice ; and is probably the form most frequently chosen for the hymn-tune. But its most important place in composition is in the larger forms, as its design adapts it peculiarly to the purposes of the themes, both principal and subordinate.

The **Three-Part Song-form,** on the contrary, is unquestionably the most common of all the music designs. Probably three-fourths of all our literature are written in this form, with or without the repetitions, or in the related Five-Part form. It is therefore difficult to enumerate the styles of composition to which this admirable design is well adapted, and for which it is employed.

The **Group-forms** will be found in many songs, études, anthems, and compositions of a fantastic, capricious, rather untrammeled character, in which freedom of expression overrules the consideration of clear, definite form. It is the design perhaps most commonly selected for the Invention, Fugue, and — particularly — the various species of Prelude ; though these styles, and others of decidedly fanciful purpose, are not unlikely to manifest approximate, if not direct, correspondence to the Three-Part Song-form. The modern Waltz is usually a group of Song-forms.

The **Song-Form with Trio** is encountered in older dances, especially the Menuetto, Passapied, Bourrée, and Gavotte (though even these are often simple Three-Part form, without Trio) ; and in many modern ones, — excepting the Waltz. It is characteristic of the March, Polonaise, modern Minuet, Gavotte and other dances, and of the Minuet — or Scherzo-movement, in sonatas and symphonies.

The **First Rondo-form** is sometimes substituted for the Song with Trio (to which it exactly corresponds in fundamental design- as we have learned) in compositions whose purpose carries them beyond the limits of the Three- or Five-Part forms, and in which greater unity, fluency and cohesion are required than can be obtained in the song with trio ; for instance, in larger Nocturnes, Romanzas, Ballades, Études, and so forth. The peculiar place for the First Rondo-form in literature, however, is in the "slow movement" (*adagio, andante, largo*) of the sonata, symphony and concerto, for which it is very commonly chosen. It may also be encountered in the *small* Rondos of a somewhat early date ; and is of course possible in broader vocal compositions (large opera, arias, anthems, etc.).

From what has just been said, the student will infer that the rondo-form is not employed exclusively in pieces that are called "Rondo." In the sense in which we have adopted the term, it applies to a *design*, and not to a style, of composition ; precisely as the sonata-allegro form may appear in a composition that is not a sonata. This must not be overlooked. Furthermore, there are a few cases in literature in which a movement maiked "Rondo" is not written according to the rondo-form.

The **Second and Third Rondo-forms** are so similar in purpose and character that they are generally applied in the same manner, with no other distinction than that of length. Besides occasional occurrence as independent compositions (for instance, the two Rondos of Beethoven, op. 51, the A minor Rondo of Mozart, the Rondos of Field, Dussek, Hummel, Czerny, etc.), these designs are most commonly utilized for the *Finale* (last movement) of the

complete sonata, concerto, string-quartet, trio, and other cham-
ber-music styles ; more rarely for the finale of the symphony.

The **Sonatine** and **Sonata-allegro Forms,** likewise, serve corresponding purposes, and are chosen according to the length or
breadth of design desired. The sonatine-form may therefore be
expected in the first movement of smaller sonatas, or sonatinas
(as they are often called), but it is not infrequently employed in
the "slow movement" of larger sonatas or symphonies.

The most distinguished of all music-designs, the sonata-allegro
form, is almost invariably chosen for the opening movement of
sonatas, symphonies, concertos, trios, string-quartets and similar
compositions, sometimes in greatly augmented dimensions. It is
also not unlikely to appear in the slow movement, and *finale,* of
the symphony.

Lesson 19. — The student may now indulge in independent re-
search, in the careful analysis of the following works :

The pianoforte sonatas of Haydn (every movement of each).

The sonatas for pianoforte and violin of Mozart, Beethoven,
Brahms, Rubinstein, Grieg, and others.

The Trios of Beethoven, Mendelssohn, Schubert.

The String-quartets (in pianoforte arrangement) of Haydn,
Mozart, Beethoven, Mendelssohn, Brahms, Schubert.

The Overtures (in pianoforte arrangement) of Mozart, Beethoven,
Weber, Cherubini.

The Concertos (pianoforte or violin) of Mozart, Beethoven,
Mendelssohn, Rubinstein, Saint-Saëns, Schumann, Grieg, Chopin.

Also a number of smaller (single) pianoforte compositions : —
the études of Chopin ; a few études of Czerny, Cramer, Clementi,
Heller ; the mazurkas, nocturnes, and préludes of Chopin ; and
miscellaneous pieces by modern writers, — Grieg, Rubinstein,
Tschaikowsky (and other Russians), Sgambati, Saint-Saëns, Mosz-
kowski, Raff, Reinecke, Scharwenka. Schütte, MacDowell, — or
any other compositions, vocal or instrumental, in which the student
may be interested, or which he may be studying.

* * *

AFTERWORD.

The expression " Musical Forms " is often used, somewhat care-lessly and erroneously, with reference to *Styles* or *Species* of com-position, instead of to the structural design upon which the music is based.   The " Barcarolle," " Mazurka," " Étude," " Anthem," and so forth, are *styles* of composition, and not necessarily identi-fied with any of the structural *designs* we have been examining. Read, again, our FOREWORD.   The general conditions which enter into the distinctions of *style* are enumerated in my " Homophonic Forms," paragraph 97, which the student is earnestly advised to read.   As to the manifold styles themselves, with which the pres-ent book is not directly concerned, the student is referred to Ernst Pauer's " Musical Forms," and to the music dictionaries of Grove, Baker, Riemann, and other standard writers, where a description of each style or species of composition may be found.

THE END.